ENGAGE THE BRAIN GAMES

MARCIA L. TATE

CORWIN PRESS
Classroom

For information:

Corwin Press
A SAGE Company
2455 Teller Road
Thousand Oaks, California 91320
CorwinPress.com

SAGE, Ltd.
1 Oliver's Yard
55 City Road
London EC1Y 1SP
United Kingdom

SAGE India Pvt. Ltd.
B 1/I 1 Mohan Cooperative
Industrial Area
Mathura Road, New Delhi
India 110 044

SAGE Asia-Pacific Pvt. Ltd.
33 Pekin Street #02-01
Far East Square
Singapore 048763

Printed in the United States of America.

ISBN: 978-1-4129-5927-8

This book is printed on acid-free paper.

08 09 10 11 12 10 9 8 7 6 5 4 3 2 1

Executive Editor: Kathleen Hex
Managing Developmental Editor: Christine Hood
Editorial Assistant: Anne O'Dell
Developmental Writer: Lori Cardoza Starnes
Developmental Editor: Heera Kang
Proofreader: Mary Barbosa
Art Director: Anthony D. Paular
Design Project Manager: Jeffrey Stith
Cover Designers: Monique Hahn and Lisa Miller
Illustrator: Corbin Hillam
Design Consultant: The Development Source

TABLE OF CONTENTS

Connections to Standards

This chart shows the national language arts standards covered in each chapter.

LANGUAGE ARTS	Standards are covered on pages
Apply a wide range of strategies to comprehend, interpret, evaluate, and appreciate texts. Draw on prior experience, interactions with other readers and writers, knowledge of word meaning and of other texts, word identification strategies, and understanding of textual features (e.g., sound-letter correspondence, sentence structure, context, graphics).	8, 12, 15, 21, 23, 27, 32, 80, 86, 93
Adjust the use of spoken, written, and visual language (e.g., conventions, style, vocabulary) to communicate effectively with a variety of audiences and for different purposes.	23, 34, 41, 44, 55, 77, 89
Employ a wide range of strategies while writing, and use different writing process elements appropriately to communicate with different audiences for a variety of purposes.	34, 48, 50
Apply knowledge of language structure, language conventions (e.g., spelling and punctuation), media techniques, figurative language, and genre to create, critique, and discuss print and nonprint texts.	27, 30, 37, 50, 55, 59, 62, 66, 70, 74, 77, 80, 86, 91
Conduct research on issues and interests by generating ideas and questions, and by posing problems. Gather, evaluate, and synthesize data from a variety of sources (e.g., print and nonprint texts, artifacts, people) to communicate discoveries in ways that suit the purpose and audience.	17, 50, 91
Develop an understanding of and respect for diversity in language use, patterns, and dialects across cultures, ethnic groups, geographic regions, and social roles.	17, 50, 82
Participate as knowledgeable, reflective, creative, and critical members of a variety of literacy communities.	21, 32, 34, 37, 41, 44, 48, 50, 59
Use spoken, written, and visual language to accomplish a purpose (e.g., for learning, enjoyment, persuasion, and the exchange of information).	12, 30, 32, 34, 37, 41, 44, 48, 50, 59, 91

Introduction

Think back to your years as a student. Which classes do you remember the most? Many of us fondly remember those dynamic classes that engaged our attention. However, we can just as easily remember those classes in which lectures seemed to last forever. The difference is that we can usually recall something we *learned* in the dynamic classroom. This is because our brains were engaged.

The latest in brain research reiterates what good teachers already know—student engagement is crucial to learning. Using various technological methods, scientists have found that the use of games to energize and engross students is one of the best strategies to activate learning. Can students truly learn content while playing games? Walk by a classroom where students are playing a game and you might see chaos at first glance. Look again—this is actually collaboration. Amidst the buzz of competition, students are willingly discussing material once considered bland. When students "play," they interact using all of their senses, stimulating brain function that helps retain content.

How to Use This Book

Correlated with the national language arts standards, this book provides a collection of games that will engage all students, even reluctant learners. The games review concepts in reading, writing, language conventions, and listening and speaking, and follow a format that promotes learning and retention, including: introduction, focus activity, modeling, guided practice, check for understanding, closing and independent practice. Using these strategies ensures that students are active participants in their own learning, not passive bystanders.

Students will learn about defining vocabulary through context clues, multiple-meaning words, root and compound words, tone and attitude in literature, literary genres, parts of speech, sentence parts, editing skills, literary devices such as metaphors and similes, and more!

Games can be fun, lively, and spirited. The little bit of extra effort it takes to implement games into your curriculum will reap loads in student involvement. You can expect high emotion, healthy rivalry, and exhilarating debate. Thus, set firm ground rules when playing any classroom game. Prepare prizes at your discretion, but typically the spirit of competition and sense of accomplishment are enough to fuel a lively game. Watch as once disinterested students transform before your eyes. Just like the fond memories of that dynamic class years ago, your students will remember the fun they had in your class and, more important, what they learned.

Put It Into Practice

Lecture and repetitive worksheets have long been the traditional method of delivering knowledge and reinforcing learning. While some higher-achieving students may engage in this type of learning, educators now know that actively engaging students' brains is not a luxury, but a necessity if students are truly to acquire and retain content, not only for tests but for life.

The 1990s were dubbed the Decade of the Brain because millions of dollars were spent on brain research. Educators today should know more about how students learn than ever before. Learnings styles theories that call for student engagement have been proposed for decades, as evidenced by research such as Howard Gardner's theory of multiple intelligences (1983), Bernice McCarthy's 4MAT Model (1990), and VAKT (visual, auditory, kinesthetic, tactile) learning styles theories.

I have identified 20 strategies that, according to brain research and learning styles theories, appear to correlate with the way the brain learns best. I have observed hundreds of teachers—regular education, special education, and gifted. Regardless of the classification or grade level of the students, exemplary teachers consistently use these 20 strategies to deliver memorable classroom instruction and help their students understand and retain vast amounts of content.

These 20 brain-based instructional strategies include the following:

1. Brainstorming and Discussion
2. Drawing and Artwork
3. Field Trips
4. Games
5. Graphic Organizers, Semantic Maps, and Word Webs
6. Humor
7. Manipulatives, Experiments, Labs, and Models
8. Metaphors, Analogies, and Similes
9. Mnemonic Devices
10. Movement
11. Music, Rhythm, Rhyme, and Rap
12. Project-based and Problem-based Instruction
13. Reciprocal Teaching and Cooperative Learning
14. Role Play, Drama, Pantomime, Charades

   978-1-4129-5927-8

15. Storytelling

16. Technology

17. Visualization and Guided Imagery

18. Visuals

19. Work Study and Apprenticeships

20. Writing and Journals

This book features Instructional Strategy 4: Games. While playing games, students use teamwork, interpersonal skills, and movement, and experience the spirit of competition. They actively express emotions, interact with friends, and explore new challenges of learning with immediate feedback and success (Beyers, 1998). The inherent joy of play is the brain's link from a world of reality to the development of creativity. In addition, play speeds up the brain's maturation process with built-in elements of competition, novelty, acknowledgement, and time limitations (Jensen, 2001).

Games involve active learning. The games in this book help students learn on a variety of levels. Some games involve quiet concentration, some energized, kinesthetic movement. However, all of the games involve interpersonal skills of sharing, discussing, creating, and working effectively with a team or partner. Once students are familiar with how a game is constructed, they can use these same ideas to create their own versions of the game. Brain research shows that when students are involved in the design and construction of a learning game, the game's effectiveness is enhanced (Wolfe, 2001).

Students are no strangers to competition. They face it regularly—vying for chair placement in orchestra, playing team sports, or auditioning for the school play. That same sense of competition and teamwork can take place in the classroom. Board games, card games, memory games, trivia games, games that encourage physicality, games that involve using the senses, and games that involve creative imagination all provide the social stimulation, discussion, movement, and creativity that make students actively participate in learning.

These memorable strategies help students make sense of learning by focusing on the ways the brain learns best. Fully supported by the latest brain research, the games presented in this resource provide the tools you need to boost motivation, energy, and most important, the academic achievement of your students.

CHAPTER 1

Reading

Context Clue Capers

Materials
- Context Clue Capers Cards reproducibles
- index cards
- scissors
- glue

Objective

Students will use a card game to learn vocabulary through context clues.

Students often skip over words they don't recognize rather than slowing down to figure out meaning. In this activity, students practice using context clues to help with difficult vocabulary by playing a Go Fish-style card game.

1. Discuss the term *context clues*. Words and phrases surrounding a difficult word can give hints about its meaning. You might find the actual definition in the context. Other context clues include synonyms, antonyms, or inferred clues.

2. Ask students to guess what the word *writhe* means. They may not know the definition of the word in isolation. Then say the sentence: *The worm wriggled and writhed its way into the ground.* From the context, we can tell the words *wriggle* and *writhe* are meant to be synonyms. Now students should have an idea of what *writhe* means. In this game, students will figure out the meaning of vocabulary words using context clues.

3. Ahead of time, photocopy and cut out the **Context Clue Capers Cards reproducibles (pages 10–11)**, and glue each card to an index card so students can't see through the paper. Each card shows an icon, such as a heart, clover, or star, and part of a sentence.

4. Divide the class into student pairs. Explain that this game is played similarly to Go Fish. The object is to get four cards with the same icon. Then players will need to unscramble the four sentence parts to create a complete sentence. After this, they guess the meaning of the underlined vocabulary word using context clues.

5. To begin, partners shuffle their set of cards, deal five cards each, and leave the rest in a facedown stack. Partners take turns asking each other for the icons they need. For example: *Do you have a flower?* Players must give up a requested card if they have it. If they don't have it, they tell their partner to pick up a card from the stack: *Go fish!*

6. Once a player has four of a kind, the game stops. He or she unscrambles the sentence parts to make a complete sentence. The player then uses context clues to guess the underlined word's meaning and writes his or her best guess on a sheet of paper. This is the player's scorecard.

7. Players then start over from the beginning until they go through each of the icons and make an attempt at defining each vocabulary word in context.

8. Pairs work together to tally their scorecards using a dictionary— one point for putting the sentence together correctly and one point for figuring out the correct definition. Players should get a point for reasonable definitions. The scoring process allows discussion about the meaning of the word.

9. Invite a volunteer to model playing the game with you. Encourage students to ask any questions they may have before they begin playing on their own.

10. To close the activity, go over the sentences again and have students analyze how they figured out the definition. Did the context clues offer a definition, synonym, antonym, or some kind of inference?

Extended Learning

Have students write sentences using the current vocabulary list in study. Ask them to break up their sentences into four parts and write each part on an index card. Then have them underline the vocabulary word and draw an icon in the corner, so the four sentence parts can be linked. Invite partners to play the game again using their handmade cards.

978-1-4129-5927-8

Context Clue Capers Cards

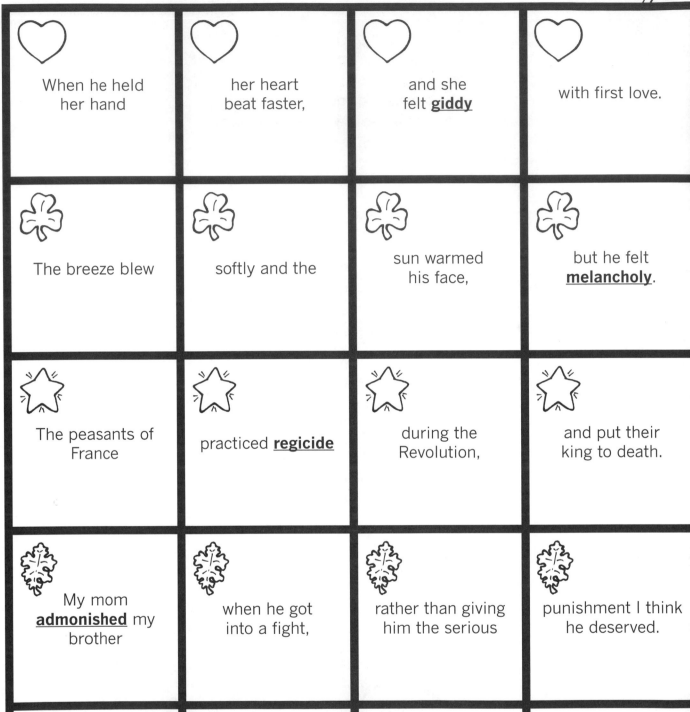

When he held her hand

her heart beat faster,

and she felt **giddy**

with first love.

The breeze blew

softly and the

sun warmed his face,

but he felt **melancholy**.

The peasants of France

practiced **regicide**

during the Revolution,

and put their king to death.

My mom **admonished** my brother

when he got into a fight,

rather than giving him the serious

punishment I think he deserved.

She plopped down the **insipid**

meal on my plate:

boiled potatoes, plain rice,

and flavorless chicken.

978-1-4129-5927-8 • © Corwin Press

Context Clue Capers Cards

☾ "Kyle is a Romeo" is	☾ an example of an **allusion**—	☾ a reference to literature,	☾ art, history, or mythology.
🍎 The **apathetic** student yawned	🍎 and doodled on	🍎 her paper during the	🍎 long, boring speech.
☺ Instead of giggling	☺ at Adina's joke,	☺ I **guffawed** loudly	☺ in the quiet library.
🐟 "Don't copy from others,"	🐟 the teacher warned. "When you	🐟 **plagiarize**, you steal someone	🐟 else's thoughts and words."
❀ I wanted to **amend** my rude	❀ comment, so I told my mother	❀ how sorry I was	❀ and asked her forgiveness.

Multiple Meanings Mania

Objective

Students will learn and review multiple meanings of vocabulary as they bluff and wager for points.

Many standardized tests pose questions about vocabulary with multiple meanings. When playing this engaging game of homographs and homophones, students practice vocabulary as well as parts of speech.

1. Write these terms on the board: *homograph* and *homophone.* Remind students that a *homograph* is a word that has the same spelling as another, but has a different meaning. A *homophone* is a word that is pronounced the same as another, but differs in spelling and meaning.

2. Ask students for two different meanings for the word *bear.* Ask for other examples of homographs. Also ask for examples of homophones, such as *night* and *knight.* Learning about homographs and homophones will help students read with understanding and do better on tests.

3. Tell students they will be playing a game using vocabulary words with multiple meanings. For the first round they will be given two homographs, along with their parts of speech. Model an example from the game by reading the first word from the **Multiple Meanings Mania reproducible (page 14)**: *bluff.* Tell students that *bluff* can be noun and a verb.

4. Ask students to think about the two meanings. Then ask a volunteer to define the noun (*a steep cliff*) and its homograph, the verb (*to mislead by a false show of strength*). Ask students to raise their hands if they knew the first meaning, then the other. Answer any questions up to this point. Ask students for other examples, such as *meet/meat, blew/blue,* and *flour/flower.*

5. Divide the class into two teams. Each team starts with 50 points. Ask a volunteer to keep score at the board.

6. Read the next homograph on the Multiple Meanings Mania reproducible and then give their parts of speech. Tell students to stand if they know both meanings of the homographs.

7. Call on a student who is standing to give the first definition, and then call on a different student to give the second definition.

8. When a student gives a correct definition, his or her team receives one point for each standing student on that team. However, only that one student need give the correct definition.

9. An element of bluffing adds excitement to the game.
   - Students can choose to stand even if they don't know the definitions. There's a chance they won't be called on, and standing helps get more points.
   - Here is the catch: If a "bluffer" answers incorrectly, the team *loses* as many points as the number of people standing. So remind them to look confident while they're bluffing!

10. Continue with the second round using homophones. This time, say and spell the word before giving the part of speech. Again, students who know both meanings should stand up. Continue reading homographs and homophones throughout the game, or ask a student volunteer to help.

11. After the game, ask students to name and define multiple-meaning words they remember from the game. Ask if they can think of additional meanings for these words.

Extended Learning
- Have students review the words from the game and write sentences using pairs of homographs or homophones. For example: *I hewed down a branch bearing flowers of a pink hue.* Allow time to share sentences in class.

- Invite students to go on a dictionary scavenger hunt! Give student pairs ten minutes to see how many words with multiple meanings they can find.

Multiple Meanings Mania

HOMOGRAPHS

bluff (noun/verb)

dress (noun/verb)

fine (noun/adjective)

flounder (noun/verb)

gag (noun/verb)

grave (noun/adjective)

loom (noun/verb)

pan (noun/verb)

prompt (noun/adjective/verb)

quail (noun/verb)

rally (noun/verb)

rash (noun/adjective)

rattle (noun/verb)

sage (noun/adjective)

short (noun/adjective)

slip (noun/verb)

slouch (noun/verb)

stalk (noun/verb)

target (noun/verb)

troop (noun/verb)

upset (noun/verb)

vault (noun/verb)

HOMOPHONES

bawled/bald (verb/adjective)

cereal/serial (noun/noun)

clause/claws (noun/noun)

cymbal/symbol (noun/noun)

discussed/disgust (verb/noun)

fowl/foul (noun/adjective)

hale/hail (adjective/verb, noun)

hue/hew (noun/verb)

idle/idol (adjective, verb/noun)

lesson/lessen (noun/verb)

meddle/medal (verb/noun)

mettle/metal (noun/noun)

minor/miner (adjective/noun)

moose/mousse (noun/noun)

pedal/peddle (noun, verb/verb)

pray/prey (verb/noun)

presents/presence (noun/noun)

rain/reign (noun, verb/noun)

roam/Rome (verb/noun)

slay/sleigh (verb/noun)

surf/serf (noun, verb/noun)

tie/Thai (noun, verb/adjective)

Joker n' Jack Attack

Objective

Students will play a game of wagering points to review text.

Materials
- deck of cards
- teacher-produced questions on a literature selection

Presenting literature in the context of a game helps students grapple with literary concepts while having fun at the same time. In this card game, students work in teams to answer questions about the literature selection. Teams wager points in order to collect the most points by the end of the game.

1. Prepare questions on a literature selection. Group the questions in three to four categories (e.g., character, plot, setting, literary devices, theme).

2. Divide the class into six teams. Rearrange desks so that teammates are facing each other, boys on one side and girls on the other. Assign a scorekeeper at the board. Each team starts with 50 points.

3. Display the following point system for each card:

   Numbered cards = that number of points

   Ace = one point

   Queens = (only girls can answer) five points

   Kings = (only boys can answer) five points

   Jacks and Jokers = Make a wager! There's no limit, but if you answer incorrectly you lose that number of points.

4. A representative from each team draws a card; the highest card starts the game. (Note: Aces are lowest and kings are highest.) The first team draws another card to determine how much their first question is worth. For example, if the player draws a seven, the question is worth seven points.

5. Model playing one round with students, and ask a prepared literature question. For example: *Name one way that setting and time affect the outcome of Catherine's life in* Catherine, Called Birdy. The team discusses their response. If they are correct, they get the points; if incorrect, they lose the points.

6. When a player draws a king or a queen, only the boys or girls on the team may discuss and answer the question.

7. When a player draws a joker or a jack, tell the team the category of the question. The team discusses and agrees on a wager before they hear the question. The team with the most points wins.

8. Play several rounds with students. After the game, ask them which questions they had the most trouble with. Review those literary concepts. The next time they play this game, challenge students to write their own questions for other subjects such as history or science.

Where on Earth?

Objective

Students will learn word derivations and definitions and review languages of the world.

In this game, students will learn about the diversity of language while reviewing geographic regions, languages, and culture. They will compete in pairs by finding word definitions, word origins, and finally researching to find new and interesting words from across the globe.

1. Write these phrases on the board:

   Paet waes god cyning!

   Smale foweles maken melodye

   Get thee to thy lady's chamber!

2. Explain that these are all English phrases—the first line Old English, the next Middle English, and finally Early Modern English. The phrases mean:

   He was a good king!

   The small birds make songs.

   Go to your girlfriend's room!

3. Tell students that English has changed significantly from its origins and has added vocabulary from parts of the world as far away as Africa, India, and the Middle East.

4. Give students a copy of the **Where on Earth? Vocabulary List** and **Abbreviated Languages reproducibles (pages 19–20)**. Review the language abbreviations with students and explain that these languages are found in most dictionaries, but there are many other ancient and modern languages. Discuss the country for each language listed. You may also wish to locate each country on a world map or atlas.

5. Divide the class into pairs. They will get 20 minutes to look in their dictionaries for as many words as possible from the Where on Earth? Vocabulary List reproducible. Before students begin, model how to find words in the dictionary as fast as possible using *guide words* at the tops of the pages.

6. Provide students with the following information:
   - Arabic pertains to the Arabian Peninsula and encapsulates the countries and ancient languages of Saudi Arabia, Jordan, Syria, Iraq, Lebanon, and North Africa.
   - Celtic and Gaelic are both languages of Ireland, Scotland, or Wales.

Materials

- Where on Earth? Vocabulary List reproducible
- Abbreviated Languages reproducible
- dictionaries
- world wall map or atlas (optional)

- Hebrew is the ancient language of the area of Israel and Palestine.
- Hindi is the official language of India.
- Nahuatl is an Aztecan language used in central Mexico.

7. Students get one point for identifying the country of origin for a word from the vocabulary list. They also get points for identifying the origin of other words in the dictionary (one point each). They will list words on the Abbreviated Languages reproducible. For example, the word *parasol* derives from Italy. Show students how to write the word *parasol* next to *Italy* on the reproducible.

8. Invite students to play the game on their own. Remind them that they have 20 minutes. When time is up, students can switch papers to add up their scores. Give them an opportunity to discuss any discrepancies about word derivations. They can go back to the dictionaries to verify answers and come to an agreement.

9. Now it's time to debrief. Ask students: *What have you learned about the English language? What words are obviously from specific countries? How do you know? What words can you already define?* Invite students to look up the meanings of unfamiliar words and share them with the class.

Extended Learning

Students may also make their own vocabulary sheets. They can browse dictionaries and find interesting words from a variety of countries to make their own lists. These lists can be used for future rounds of the game.

978-1-4129-5927-8

Name _____   Date _____

Where on Earth? Vocabulary List

Directions: Using a dictionary, find the country of origin for each word.

apartheid _____	ketchup _____
azure _____	monsoon _____
bangle _____	parasol _____
banjo _____	quatrain _____
bizarre _____	renegade _____
boomerang _____	safari _____
boycott _____	sandal _____
cartoon _____	shampoo _____
chili _____	silk _____
chipotle _____	slurp _____
chocolate _____	tofu _____
decoy _____	tornado _____
flamingo _____	tycoon _____
fuchsia _____	vendetta _____
grenade _____	verandah _____
grotesque _____	wiggle _____
hazard _____	Yankee _____
jasmine _____	yogurt _____
kangaroo _____	zombie _____

Abbreviated Languages

Directions: Using a dictionary, find words that originate from the following regions.

Language	Abbreviation	Words
Arabic	Ar.	
Celtic	Celt	
Chinese	Chin.	
Danish	Dan.	
English	E.	
French	Fr.	
Gaelic	Gael.	
German	Ger.	
Greek	Gk.	
Hebrew	Heb.	
Hindi	Hindi	
Iranian	Iran.	
Irish	Ir.	
Italian	Ital.	
Japanese	J.	
Nahuatl	Nahuatl	
Persian	Pers.	
Polish	Pol.	
Portuguese	Port.	
Romanian	Rom.	
Russian	Russ.	
Scandinavian	Scand.	
Scots	Sc.	
Spanish	Sp.	

The Root of the Matter

Materials
• index cards
• colored markers
• dictionaries

Objective
Students will learn Greek and Latin word roots and use this knowledge to form new vocabulary words.

The roots of Greek and Latin appear in thousands of words students use every day. Word roots can be the key to unlocking meaning in new vocabulary. In this game, students create cards containing Greek and Latin roots and compete to form vocabulary words using these roots. By drawing, sharing, discussing, and then competing with self-made game cards, students retain knowledge and build vocabulary. This game can be divided into two class sessions if necessary.

1. Tell students that the English words they use daily have Greek and Latin roots. Give some examples using the roots and meanings provided below (e.g., *automobile, biography, bicycle, dictionary*).

2. For the first part of this game, students will create and study word root flashcards. Write the following roots on the board (add more roots, if desired). Give students colored markers and index cards. Have them write a word root on one side of the cards and on the other side draw a picture that hints at the meaning of the root. For example, for *crat/cracy*, students could draw a crown.

Sample Word Root List

Root	Meaning
auto	self
bio	life
crat/cracy	rule
cycl/cyclo	wheel, circular
dict	speak, say
fac/fact/fic	do, make
loc/loco	place
mar/mari/mer	sea
mem	remember
phon	sound
port	carry
sent/sens	feel
tele	far
uni	one
vac	empty
vid/vis	see

3. After students finish their cards, erase the board. Have student pairs switch flashcards. Allow time for students to study the cards by trying to remember the word root meanings using the illustrated hints on the cards.

4. Start the game by calling out one root at a time. Players will brainstorm as many words as possible using the root. Give points to the pair with the most words for each root in a designated amount of time. Assign a "referee" to look up contested words in a dictionary. The winners will have the most overall points.

5. The next part of this game is played like a TV game show. Separate the class into groups of three to play a mock game show using their word root flashcards. Students can take turns being the game show host, while the other two compete against each other.

6. Using one student's set of flashcards, the "host" will first read the root and then show the drawing on the flashcard as a hint. The first player to think of the meaning of the root raises a hand. The player must give the meaning of the root and a word that contains the root.

7. The host uses a dictionary to check contested words. If the first player cannot think of a word containing the root, the other player gets a chance. Players get one point for the meaning and one point for the vocabulary word containing the root.

8. Next, players move on to the final round. Each player takes a turn. The host gives a root and its meaning, and the player gets 30 seconds to call out as many words as possible containing that root. The third student records the words. Each word earns one point.

9. Before students begin playing on their own, model several rounds with the help of volunteers. For example: **Auto** means "self"; *automobile*. Check to make sure students understand how to proceed with the game. Then allow them to play in teams while you circulate around the room and assist as needed.

10. After the game, discuss with the class any new words they have learned. Invite them to share new words they thought were particularly original.

Synonym Shades and Grades

Objective

Students will play a sorting activity to analyze the subtle differences in meaning and tone between synonyms.

Materials
• Synonym Sets reproducibles
• dictionaries
• 2–4 paper lunch bags

There is more to a synonym than its definition—a word having the same or nearly the same meaning as another word. In this activity, students work together to study the gradation of synonyms. They will learn the nuances of similar-meaning words that give each synonym its own flavor.

1. Write one set of synonyms from the **Synonym Sets reproducibles (pages 25–26)** on the board. Ask students: *Do these words mean the same thing? Although they might be listed as synonyms in a thesaurus, they do not have the same exact meaning or effect.*

2. For example, ask students these questions to illustrate slight differences between synonyms: *Would you rather get a Valentine from someone whose feelings are caring, loving, or passionate? Would you rather eat something that's tasty, appetizing, or delicious?* Word choice, or diction, is extremely important in conveying exact meaning.

This sandwich is ~~tasty~~ ~~appetizing~~ delicious!

3. Cut out the sets of synonyms on the Synonym Sets reproducibles. Place the sets in separate paper bags.

4. Divide the class into teams of nine students each. Give each group a set of synonyms. To play the game, each player draws a synonym from the bag. He or she looks up the definition of the synonym and tells teammates what it means. Players will need to understand the fine differences between each synonym.

5. To begin, ask groups to stand up and arrange themselves in a line in the order described below. A time limit is optional.
   Set 1: From the least intelligent to the most (i.e., the word that means "smartest")
   Set 2: From the least red to the most
   Set 3: From the least sleepy to the most
   Set 4: From the least happy to the most
   Set 5: From the least scary to the most
   Set 6: From the least unpleasant to the most
   Set 7: From the least amount of rainfall to the most
   Set 8: From the least intense feeling to the most

6. After teams have arranged themselves the best they can, going down the line, players must say a few sentences describing "who they are" and how they are different from the players standing next to them.

7. Model the first synonym, *brilliant*, for students. For example: *I am "brilliant." I am the most intelligent one in this group. I am all of the others combined.* Next, invite a volunteer to model the next word, *intelligent*. For example: *I am "intelligent." I can understand things quickly and have a high mental ability. But I wouldn't say I am "brilliant." That's a whole different level.*

8. Invite students to play with the remaining sets of synonyms. Make sure students understand that there are no right answers in this activity. The most important goal is to be able to differentiate one synonym from another.

9. After the game, ask students why they put the synonyms in the order they did. For example, why might they have thought that *crimson* was lighter than *scarlet*? Allow students to articulate their thoughts by providing examples, justifications, and specifics in their definitions.

Extended Learning

- Ask students to choose their favorite excerpts from various literature selections. Have them decide which words they feel have the strongest connotation, or feelings surrounding the word. Take out that word and insert a synonym. Ask students: *How has the meaning of the sentence changed? How has the author's purpose shifted? Which sentence is better? Why?*

- Invite students to use thesauruses to find and create their own synonym sets. Have them exchange sets with other groups and play more rounds of the game.

Synonym Sets

jovial	comatose	lazy	burgundy	proficient	brilliant
comical	dreamy	slothful	fuchsia	intelligent	clever
blithe	tired	unenergetic	ruby	bright	quick
jocund	silly	sluggish	rose	coral	sharp
funny	hilarious	lethargic	red	crimson	wise
good-humored	merry	indolent	maroon	scarlet	smart

Synonym Sets

loving	amorous	romantic	admiring	affectionate	fond
precipitation	torrent	downpour	caring	passionate	ardent
mist	drizzle	tempest	shower	rain	sprinkle
heinous	vile	gross	repulsive	icky	objectionable
frightful	ghostly	deathly	foul	disgusting	repugnant
eerie	creepy	spooky	ghoulish	gruesome	ominous

Compound It!

Objective

Students will learn and remember compound words by playing a class game played similarily to the popular commercial game *Concentration®* (a registered trademark of NBC Universal, Inc.).

Materials
• Compound It! Word List reproducibles
• scissors

Most students have played this matching game with pictures since they were young. In this twist on the original game, students will find and put together separate words to make compound words.

1. Review with students that a compound word is made up of two or more words. For example: *watermelon, underwater, wildlife*. Ask students for other examples and list them on the board. Tell students that they will be playing a game similar to Concentration® to review compound words.

2. Give a copy of the **Compound It! Word List reproducibles (pages 28–29)** to each student pair. Ask students to cut out the word cards, mix them up, and lay them facedown on a desk or table.

3. Remind students how to play the game. Each player turns over two words. If the two words make a compound word, he or she keeps the words. If the words do not make a compound word, the player places the words facedown in their original positions.

4. Show students how to make a compound word with the word cards. For example, if you flip over the word card *air*, it can be paired with *craft* to create a compound word. Explain that play continues until all words are matched. The player who makes the most compound words (possesses the most word cards) wins the game.

5. After the game, ask students to revisit their compound words. Invite them to find out what each individual word means, and then what the words mean when they are combined to make a compound word. For example, what do the words *spell* and *bound* mean? What does the compound word *spellbound* mean?

air | craft   clock | wise

back | fire

Compound It! Word List

air	craft	back
fire	black	top
clock	wise	cob
web	cow	boy
cross	walk	day
dream	draw	bridge
drive	way	eye
sore	finger	print
folk	lore	frame

Reproducible

Compound It! Word List

work	grave	stone
wrist	watch	head
strong	keep	sake
loop	hole	main
stream	out	standing
quarter	back	safe
guard	spell	bound
wind	shield	home
sick	earth	quake

Snow Day

Materials
- white paper, cut in half
- large box

Objective

Students will create their own review game using vocabulary, figurative language, parts of speech, or literary elements.

Studying for tests doesn't have to be painful. This game is a cross between dodge ball and an invigorating indoor snowball fight! Students will enjoy hurling "snowballs" that contain a variety of questions to help them review concepts.

1. Begin by reminding students that they can do better on tests when they're prepared to answer a variety of different types of questions. Explain that they will be creating questions for a game. Brainstorm some of the different types of questions they have seen on tests and write these on the board. For example: *multiple choice, true/false, fill in the blank, short answer, summarize, solve, explain, compare/contrast, analyze.*

2. Choose a literature selection. Review the concepts students have learned (e.g., parts of speech, plot, character, setting, figurative language, vocabulary) and write them on the board.

3. Ask students to choose three question types from the board. They will write one question for each type and number them *1, 2, 3*, from easiest to hardest. The questions should deal with a concept listed on the board. Circulate around the room checking for questions that are too basic or too confusing.

   Following are examples of numbers *1, 2,* and *3* questions from the book *The Outsiders* by S. E. Hinton:
   1. The two brothers of Ponyboy Curtis are _____ and _____.
   2. What is the event that leads to Johnny Cade's huge problem?
   3. Compare and contrast the Greasers and the Socs. Name three similarities and three differences.

4. Divide the class into four teams, and have each team stand in a corner of the classroom. (As an alternative, play the game outside.) Place the box in the center of the room.

5. Have students crumple their papers into "snowballs." Make sure they keep track of the question numbers.

6. Team 1 hurls their number *1* snowballs at Team 2. When the questions stop flying, players on Team 2 pick up the snowballs closest to them and read the questions aloud, one player at a time. If the player can answer the question, then he or she stays

standing. If not, that player must sit down and give his or her snowball to a teammate. Place the snowballs players could not answer into the box in the middle of the room.

7. After playing one practice round to make sure students understand the directions, invite them to continue playing. This time, Team 2 throws their number *1* questions at Team 3, and so on, until all the questions have been thrown and answers have been attempted. The team with the most members standing after three rounds wins the game.

8. After the game, read aloud the unanswered questions in the box. Ask the class for possible answers, and provide some clues if needed. Discuss which questions were the most difficult and why. Talk about the variety of questions and why some take more brainpower than others.

Extended Learning

Use a similar concept for spelling review. Divide the class into small teams and read aloud a spelling word. Have teams write the word on a piece of paper, crumple it up, and toss it into the box. Have a volunteer read and spell aloud each word to check for correctness. The team with the most correct answers wins the game!

Around the World

Materials
• teacher-generated literature questions or vocabulary/spelling list

Objective

Students will play a game of quick thinking and articulation to review concepts in literature or to build vocabulary and spelling skills.

This game can be used to review a variety of language arts concepts, including literature, vocabulary, and spelling. Students will be challenged to quickly think of correct answers to achieve points, gain territory, and review information. This activity encourages even the shyest students to get actively involved.

1. Explain that this game is called *Around the World* because students will travel from desk to desk as they compete against each other. The "traveler" who makes it completely around the classroom or "world" wins the game.

2. Indicate that there may be two winners—the traveler who reaches the last desk and the traveler who moves the farthest to rack up the most points.

3. Assign a scorekeeper to keep track of how many times a traveler moves from desk to desk. Simply have the scorekeeper write each traveler's name and number of correct responses.

4. Position all desks in a circle, or you may choose a path around the classroom for travelers to follow. Ask for a volunteer to model the game and become the first traveler. Explain the rules of the game while students begin playing:
   a. The traveler stands next to the first desk. Ask a question about either literature, the spelling of a word, or a vocabulary word definition. The first student in the pair (the traveler or the student sitting at the desk) to raise his or her hand gets the chance to respond.

b. If the traveler is first and responds correctly, he or she moves on to the next desk. If the traveler is incorrect, the sitting student gets a chance to answer. If that student is correct, he or she becomes the new traveler and the former traveler sits at the desk. If that student is also incorrect, the student at the next desk becomes the new traveler.

c. The traveler who makes it to the last desk wins the game. The other winner, determined by the scorekeeper, is the student who moved the most times and accumulated the most points, even if he or she did not make it to the last desk.

5. After modeling a couple of rounds of questions, invite students to begin "traveling"! During play, urge students to use good sportsmanship and to encourage their classmates.

6. To close the activity, play one final round in which you ask three questions of the two winners to determine a final winner.

Extended Learning

• Invite students to work in groups to research and write questions to play additional rounds of Around the World.

• Use this game for review before a test.

CHAPTER 2

Writing

Paper Prison

Materials
- Paper Prison Writing Constraints reproducible
- gag gift (e.g., birthday party hat, oversized sunglasses)

Objective

Students will write with more clarity and description as they practice writing conventions.

A few simple strategies can help make students' writing clearer, more colorful, and significantly more interesting. In this game, students learn how to free their writing from the shackles of weak verbs, ineffective punctuation, and simple sentences.

1. Choose an enjoyable journal topic for a "quick write." Some examples include: *Write about the meaning of your name. Describe the world from the viewpoint of a germ. Do you believe in love at first sight?*

2. Then have students switch papers with a partner and count the number of "to be" verbs in their partner's writing. Prepare a gag gift for the "winner."

3. Explain that "to be" verbs add little meaning to a sentence. Ask students: *What do the words **is** and **are** mean?* Students will have a difficult time coming up with an answer. Point out that the verb *to be* joins together subjects and verbs but does not add any meaning to the sentence.

4. Tell students that the first round of this writing competition involves eliminating "to be" verbs. By doing this, they add clarity to their writing.

"To Be" Verbs
am
are
is
was
were
be
become
became

5. Discuss the difficulties of writing within a constraint—it's like a paper prison, trapped by word shackles. Explain that the easiest way to break free from "to be" verbs is to use action verbs instead. Provide students with a couple of examples, such as: *The ghost was eerie and next to the tombstone* could be changed to *The eerie ghost floated next to the tombstone.*

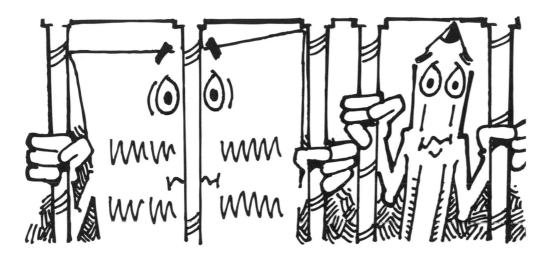

6. Give students 10–15 minutes to write. Have them describe a scary place using as few "to be" verbs as possible. Explain that this time the winner will be the student who uses the least "to be" verbs and the most action verbs.

7. Again, have students switch papers with a partner and count the action verbs. After determining the winners (you may choose to award first, second, and third places), invite them to share their paragraphs with the class.

8. Tell students that for round two, they will write with a different type of constraint from the **Paper Prison Writing Constraints reproducible (page 36)**. Continue with more rounds of the game, using constraints listed on the reproducible. Ask students to reflect on which constraint was the most difficult. Allow more time for students to practice writing with the constraints they found most difficult.

Extended Learning

Have students share sentences that they had the most difficulty writing without "to be" verbs. They can work in pairs to brainstorm action verbs for these sentences.

Paper Prison Writing Constraints

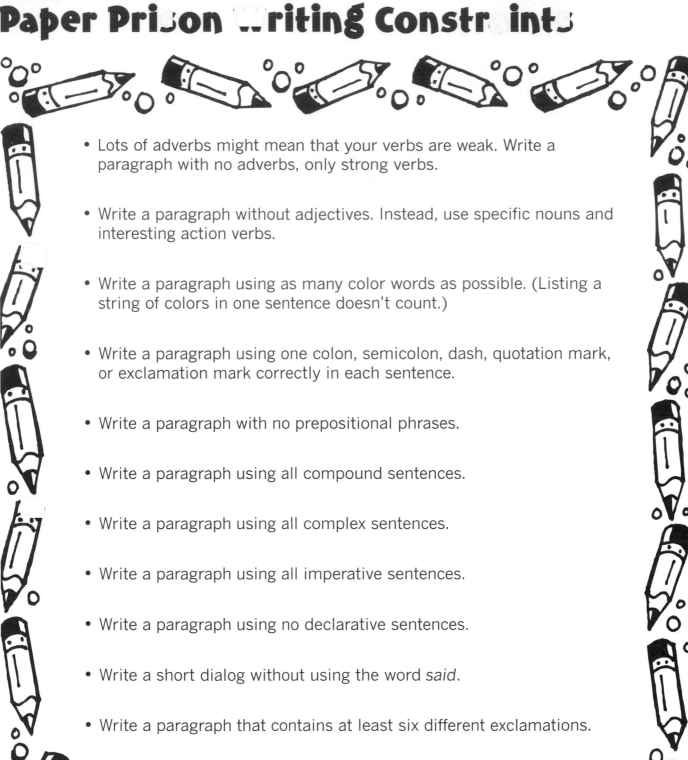

- Lots of adverbs might mean that your verbs are weak. Write a paragraph with no adverbs, only strong verbs.

- Write a paragraph without adjectives. Instead, use specific nouns and interesting action verbs.

- Write a paragraph using as many color words as possible. (Listing a string of colors in one sentence doesn't count.)

- Write a paragraph using one colon, semicolon, dash, quotation mark, or exclamation mark correctly in each sentence.

- Write a paragraph with no prepositional phrases.

- Write a paragraph using all compound sentences.

- Write a paragraph using all complex sentences.

- Write a paragraph using all imperative sentences.

- Write a paragraph using no declarative sentences.

- Write a short dialog without using the word *said*.

- Write a paragraph that contains at least six different exclamations.

- Write a paragraph about a race without using the words *run* or *ran*.

- Write a paragraph that includes references to all five senses at least twice.

Couplet Chaos

Objective

Students will compete to produce creative couplets and quatrains.

Materials
- Couplet Chaos Team Starters reproducible
- Couplet Chaos Game Starters reproducible
- timer

Playing a game can ease some of the anxiety students may have about reading and writing poetry. In this game, students will determine the characteristics of different forms of poetry. Then they will write their own structured poems.

1. Write the following couplets on the board:

   I have the measles and the mumps,

   A gash, a rash, and purple bumps.

   —Shel Silverstein

   One kiss, my bonny sweetheart, I'm after a prize to-night,

   But I shall be back with the yellow gold before the morning light;

   —Alfred Noyes

   Love looks not with the eyes, but with the mind;

   And therefore is winged Cupid painted blind.

   —William Shakespeare

   She had, the guide informed him later,

   Been eaten by an alligator.

   —Ogden Nash

2. Ask students: *What do you notice about these couplets? What makes them unique?* Then ask: *What are some alternative endings for the first lines of poetry? What other rhymes could be used to change meaning?* Share other couplets from literature students may be reading.

3. Explain that a couplet is two successive lines of verse that rhyme at the end and are about the same length. Then describe a quatrain: a stanza (section of poetry) with four lines. Two couplets that make sense together make a quatrain. Share the Ogden Nash couplet finished as a quatrain:

   She had, the guide informed him later,

   Been eaten by an alligator.

   Professor Twist could not but smile.

   "You mean," he said, "a crocodile."

4. Cut a copy of the **Couplet Chaos Team Starters reproducible (page 39)** into strips and give a strip to each student. Invite students to search for their partners by matching rhymes and making couplets. Each couplet pair must then find another couplet pair to form a sensible quatrain. These quatrains make a team of four. Model how to match up one or two couplets from the reproducible.

5. Next, have each "quatrain" sit together. Read or display a line from the **Couplet Chaos Game Starters reproducible (page 40)**. In two to three minutes, teams should complete the couplet with as many appropriate and sensible rhyming lines as possible.

6. Determine with a show of hands which teams have the most answers. Read the top two teams' answers. Only couplets that make sense should be counted.

7. The game can be repeated several times. The next level of play is the quatrain level. With more time, teams will use the first lines of the Game Starters reproducible to write as many quatrains as they can. The team with the most quatrains wins the game.

8. Close the activity by asking students to vote on the funniest, most unique, or most clever rhymes.

Couplet Chaos Team Starters

Halloween ghouls haunt
in the black night,

Wailing and shrieking with
a tortured fright.

Halloween's hues are black and gold;

It's the season when eerie tales unfold.

The spaceship landed in a field of corn;

It's where the Martian Areo was born.

He had twelve eyes on his big green face;

It's how we figured he was
from outer space.

Romeo loved the fair Juliet,

But didn't like her last name, Capulet.

Their families had many feuds and hate,

But Romeo wooed Juliet,
sealing their fate.

Snakes have no external ears.

They cannot hear your laughter or tears.

A snake charmer's music would
have no sound;

His movements, instead, hold
snakes spellbound.

In Australia, they like their
burgers with beets.

While in England, pea pudding
is what locals eat.

To New Zealanders,
iced tea is often disdained;

"Like drinking hot cola," is how
it's explained.

Madagascar cockroaches have no wings;

They use hisses for
communicating things.

They hiss in a fight;
they hiss when they greet;

They hiss when there are new
girlfriends to meet.

Antarctica, though filled
with ice and snow

Is considered a desert because
precipitation is low.

In this land of ice, moisture cannot hold

Because of the air's harsh, deadly cold.

In the real story from Brothers Grimm,

Cinderella's tale isn't nearly as prim.

The stepsister saws off a
chunk of her heel

To fit into that shoe! What
a bloody ordeal!

Couplet Chaos Game Starters

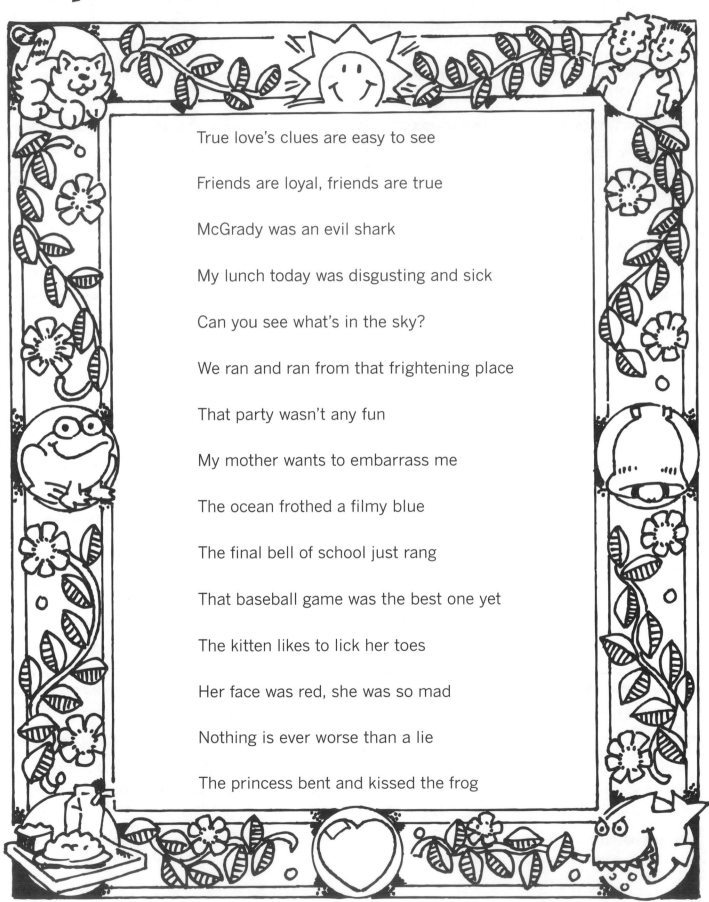

True love's clues are easy to see

Friends are loyal, friends are true

McGrady was an evil shark

My lunch today was disgusting and sick

Can you see what's in the sky?

We ran and ran from that frightening place

That party wasn't any fun

My mother wants to embarrass me

The ocean frothed a filmy blue

The final bell of school just rang

That baseball game was the best one yet

The kitten likes to lick her toes

Her face was red, she was so mad

Nothing is ever worse than a lie

The princess bent and kissed the frog

Reproducible 978-1-4129-5927-8 • © Corwin Press

Tone It Up

Objective

Students will learn about tone and attitude in literature by first brainstorming words that convey tone and then rewriting nursery rhymes with a new attitude.

Materials
• copies of nursery rhymes

Tone is an abstract concept. It is defined as the writer's attitude toward the subject, but it is often confused with effect. The effect of a piece may be humorous, but the tone may be angry, even as we laugh at the speaker's ire.

In this game, students brainstorm words that convey tone. They will try to find at least one word that starts with each letter of the alphabet. This list will help students with what comes next in the activity— changing tone in familiar nursery rhymes.

1. Explain the concepts of *tone* and *attitude* in literature. Ask students: *What does someone mean when he or she says, "I don't like your tone"?*

2. Invite student volunteers to say this line aloud: *It's so expensive.* Ask them to say it in a delighted tone, a disgusted tone, a surprised tone, and a disappointed tone. Make sure to emphasize the fact that the words are the same, only the attitude has changed.

3. To check for understanding, read some sample lines of poetry or literature and ask students to describe the tone. There may be more than one correct idea. Compare the tone in the following poem by William Blake to the tone in the last lines of Brothers Grimm's *Cinderella*.

"The Sick Rose" by William Blake

O Rose, thou art sick!
The invisible worm
That flies in the night,
In the howling storm,

Has found out thy bed
Of crimson joy;
And his dark secret love
Does thy life destroy.

Last Lines of *Cinderella* by the Brothers Grimm

"When the betrothed couple went to church, the elder [stepsister] was at the right side and the younger at the left, and the pigeons pecked out one eye of each of them. Afterwards as they came back, the elder was at the left, and the younger at the right, and then the pigeons pecked out the other eye of each. And thus, for their wickedness and falsehood, they were punished with blindness as long as they lived."

4. After discussing students' responses, explain that the tone of "The Sick Rose" may be deemed eerie, haunting, or horrific. However, while the effect of the *Cinderella* piece might be similar, the author's attitude is not. The tone of that piece is matter-of-fact, objective, or detached.

Sample Tone Word List

accusing	fanciful	proud
admiring	flattered	restrained
angry	frivolous	sarcastic
apologetic	giddy	silly
arrogant	humorous	somber
bitter	incredulous	sweet
bland	ironic	threatening
bored	irreverent	tolerant
cold	joyful	tragic
complimentary	kind	upset
condescending	lighthearted	urgent
detached	loving	vexed
dramatic	matter-of-fact	vibrant
dreamy	mocking	witty
eager	nostalgic	worried
evasive	objective	zealous

---

5. Now that students have some idea of tone and tone words, group them into teams of three to four. Ask students to write the letters of the alphabet vertically down a sheet of paper. Give them five to ten minutes to list as many tone words as possible. Although the team works together, students should write ideas on their own paper, so they will all have their own list of alphabetized tone words.

6. Teams will get two points for the first tone word for each letter and one point for additional words starting with that letter. For

example, for *A*, they get two points for their first answer *(annoyed)* but only one for the next *(affectionate)*.

7. Ask students to count their points. Have the two-top scoring teams switch papers and read aloud their answers. The class should judge if they are truly tone words. Students can add new words to their own lists as they hear the answers.

8. Next, hand out copies of nursery rhymes to students and explain that they will rewrite them using a specific tone. Students can work alone or in teams. Have students look through their list and choose a tone and a nursery rhyme to rewrite.

9. Model this activity with students by rewriting a nursery rhyme together. Explain that word choice often determines tone. For example, to create an apathetic tone, "Little Miss Muffet" can be changed in the following way:

    Little Miss Muffet

    Lounged on her tuffet

    Sighing over cold oatmeal.

    Along came a spider

    Who tried to affright her

    But she yawned, asking, "What's your deal?"

10. Ask students to think of multiple-choice answers to the question: *What is the tone?* For the above example, answers could be: *a. horrific, b. tragic, c. apathetic, d. loving, e. threatening.*

11. Ask students to come to the front of the classroom, one at a time. Have them read aloud their revised "tone poems," and ask their multiple-choice question. The rest of the class will write their answers on a separate sheet of paper, including the name of the writer and the multiple-choice answer. The student with the most correct answers wins!

12. Close this activity by asking students to vote on who wrote the nursery rhyme that was the funniest, cleverest, or most interesting; used the best word choices; had the most obvious tone; and so on.

Extended Learning

Remind students of this assignment the next time they read a text. Ask them to think about tone when they read their science book, a cereal box, a comic strip, or a novel for class. Explain that the more they practice figuring out the tone in writing, the easier it becomes.

Pass, Write, and Edit

Materials

- Pass, Write, Edit Story Frame reproducibles
- 35+ pictures of people cut from magazines and glued to construction paper
- highlighter markers

Objective

Students will write cooperative stories based on pictures, and then edit their stories for mechanical errors.

Students should know that even the best writers rely on editors to help them write clear and engaging pieces. In this activity, not only will students write a character sketch, they will also act as editors, competing to see who has the perfectly written tale.

1. Tell students that good writing is a combination of creativity and form (e.g., diction, grammar, spelling). Ask them to think about an artist who has a great idea for a painting. If the artist doesn't practice his or her skills, the painting will end up being a disappointment and nowhere near what the artist had imagined. In the same way, writers need to refine their skills in order to convey clearly the ideas in their minds.

2. Give each student one picture and a copy of the **Pass, Write, Edit Story Frame reproducibles (pages 46–47)**. Place students into teams of four or five, and invite team members to sit in a circle.

3. Ask students to look at their picture and complete the first statement, using their imagination and clues from the picture. There are no "right" answers. Students should concentrate on creating specific, detailed responses.

4. When finished with the first statement, students pass both their picture and papers to the student on the right. Everyone should have a new picture and the reproducibles. The next student then reviews the picture and their teammate's writing before completing the next statement.

 978-1-4129-5927-8

5. Have students continue passing pictures and papers until all statements are completed.

6. Explain to students that the winner of this writing competition is the team that makes the fewest grammatical errors in their stories. Each team gets five minutes to edit, correct, and discuss their stories.

7. After papers are completed, tell teams to exchange papers. Each student gets a highlighter marker for marking errors and a story to edit. They may ask teammates for help.

8. Before students begin, review the errors each editor should look for. Write this editing checklist on the board:
   - general punctuation
   - spelling
   - comma placement, including dates and lists
   - capitalization (e.g., names of people and places, holidays, proper nouns)
   - book and movie titles underlined
   - proper use of quotation marks

9. Have editors add up the errors. Ask one person from each team to gather the papers and return them to the original writers. Then each team counts their collective errors. If anyone disagrees with an edit on his or her paper, he or she discusses the issue with the team. If there is still disagreement, have the student write the sentence on the board and reach a class consensus. Ask teams to raise their hands as you count down the number of errors until one team is left—the winners!

10. To close the activity, invite students to rewrite their stories on another sheet of paper. Ask them to use editing marks to correct any errors. Collect students' finished products in order to assess their progress.

Extended Learning

Have students use the Pass, Write, Edit Story Frame to write a biography about a classmate. Ask students to use the editing skills they learned. Allow time for them to share their biographies with the class.

Name _____ Date _____

Pass, Write, Edit Story Frame 1

Directions: Look at the picture and use your imagination to complete one item. Then pass your paper and picture to the person on your right. Be creative and specific!

1. This is (name) _____.

2. He/She was born on (date) _____.

3. His/Her favorite things in the world are (name four things):

_____

_____

_____

_____

4. He/She used to be _____, but now

_____

_____.

5. He/She loves the book _____ because

_____

_____.

6. His/Her favorite quote is _____ because

_____.

7. He/She works at _____ because

_____

Name _____ Date _____

Pass, Write, Edit Story Frame 2

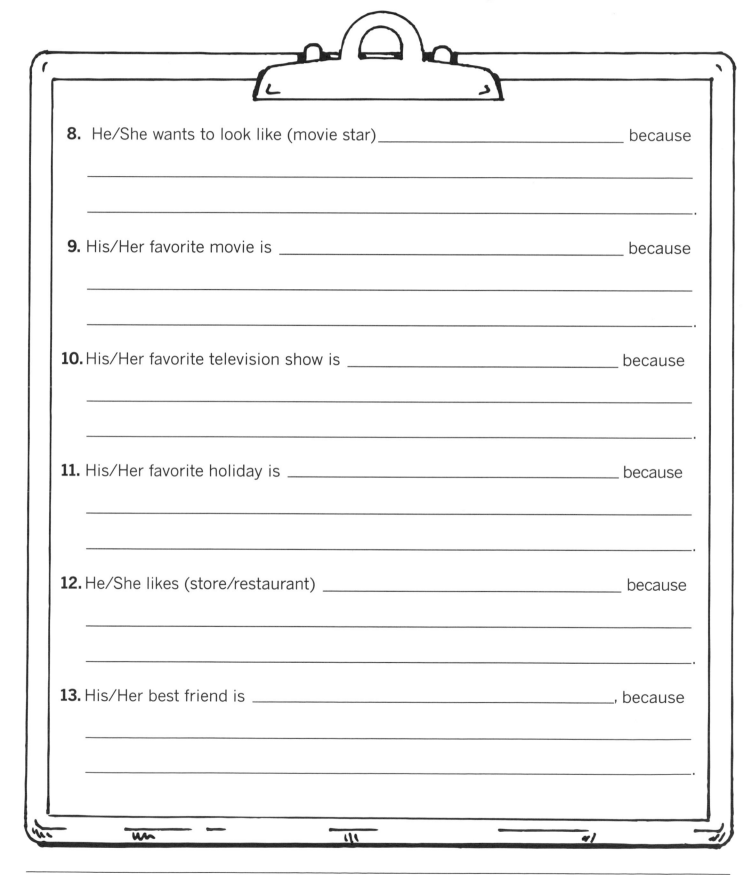

8. He/She wants to look like (movie star) _____ because

_____

_____ .

9. His/Her favorite movie is _____ because

_____

_____ .

10. His/Her favorite television show is _____ because

_____

_____ .

11. His/Her favorite holiday is _____ because

_____

_____ .

12. He/She likes (store/restaurant) _____ because

_____

_____ .

13. His/Her best friend is _____, because

_____

_____

Story Scrambles

Materials
- index cards with elements of plot written on them
- 5–10 magazines
- construction paper
- scissors
- glue

Objective
Students will learn the elements of plot while they write and share stories.

Students enjoy creating silly stories using fun and engaging pictures for inspiration. This game combines kinesthetic and interpersonal skills to help students remember the parts of a plotline.

1. Review the elements of a plotline: exposition, conflict, rising action, climax, and resolution. Write the following on the board:

   Exposition: *the beginning part of a story, the setting, and the characters*

   Conflict: *the main problem*

   Rising Action: *the events that add to the problem*

   Climax: *the most intense part of the story; the major turning point*

   Resolution/Denouement: *the events that end or solve the problem*

2. Using a story most students know, such as *Jack and the Beanstalk*, have students name the elements of the plot. Ask them how they were able to identify each part of the story.

3. Pass out magazines, construction paper, scissors, and glue. Ask students to find an action-packed scene from a magazine and glue it onto construction paper. The scene should include at least one person. The more exciting, the better! (As an alternative, prepare these ahead of time.)

4. Prepare a class set of index cards. On each card, write one element of plot, making sure there are equal numbers of each element. If there are extra cards, write *rising action* on them. Shuffle the cards and hand each student an index card.

   978-1-4129-5927-8

5. Then ask a student to count off one through five, and assign each student a number to a plot element, such as *exposition–1, conflict–2, rising action–3, climax–4,* and *resolution–5.*

6. Explain that this is a game of quick thinking and imagination. Tell students that they will be judged and evaluated on the development of character(s), interesting conflict, action, an exciting climax, a creative resolution, vivid verbs, and specific or sensory details.

7. To begin, students circulate around the room and try and find other students to complete a plotline. (A group may have more than one *rising action.*) Once a group has all five elements, they take the first picture from the stack of magazine clippings.

8. As quickly as possible, students create a story using the picture as inspiration. Each student is responsible for writing his or her plot element for the story on a separate sheet of paper. Following is the only discussion groups are allowed to have:
   • Agree on the characters' names
   • Agree on the characters' relationships to each other, if there is more than one person in the picture
   • Agree on the general setting—in five words or less, where does the story (as shown in the picture) take place?

9. Hold up a magazine picture and model how to develop a character and setting from the elements shown. Ask students to help you with ideas to further develop your writing.

10. Give students the signal to begin writing. After discussion, students must be silent and write on their own. The idea is that, in the end, they will have an interesting, zany story (but one that includes all elements of plot) based on the same picture. The first team to finish raises their hands. Once the second team is done, then all writing stops.

11. Invite both teams to read their stories aloud, each student reading his or her part of the plot. Then allow the class to vote for their favorite story.

12. After the game, students can talk about which part of the plotline they most liked writing and why. Repeat the game several times as time permits.

Genre Jumble

Objective

Students will research the tenets and vocabulary of literary genres and use the information to rewrite a melodrama.

Students will enjoy learning about literary genres when they are allowed to write, direct, and act out a short play of their own. In this game, students use vocabulary, props, and given situations to rewrite a play and teach the rest of the class the tenets of a genre.

Materials
- "Genre Jumble" Elements Chart reproducible
- Dante the Dastardly reproducibles
- library or computer access

1. Write the term *genre* on the board. Underneath, list these words: *stock characters, plot elements, props/settings, dialect/ vocabulary,* and *miscellaneous.* Explain that a literary genre is a type or style of story. Ask students to consider sections of a bookstore and how the books are categorized. Brainstorm genres such as *western, horror, mystery, science fiction, romance,* and *fantasy.*

2. Define the term *melodrama.* The genre of old-fashioned melodrama includes stock characters (or the usual characters)—a damsel in distress, a righteous hero, and an evil villain. Other tenets are exaggerated emotions, overly dramatic music, good triumphing over evil, preposterous coincidences, and a happy ending. Explain that melodramas were considered "saloon entertainment"—shallow, fun, and corny. Write these ideas under the proper headings on the board.

3. Ask students what modern movies or television shows still have many of the elements of a melodrama. Consider the elements of TV shows (such as soap operas) or films (such as *King Kong*).

4. Give students a copy of the **"Genre Jumble" Elements Chart** and **Dante the Dastardly reproducibles (pages 52–54)**. Ask for volunteers to read the play aloud, while overemphasizing the corny, melodramatic aspects. As a class, discuss and fill in the chart, explaining how this play fulfills the genre's requirements.

5. Place students in groups of four or five, and assign each group one of the genres you brainstormed earlier. Then ask groups to research their genres using the library and the Internet. Instruct them to type the genre into a search engine, such as *western,* but also to look up *literary genre* as well. They should become experts on this genre and complete their "Genre Jumble" Elements Chart with as much information as they can find. Assist students as needed.

6. Afterwards, give groups time to rewrite "Dante the Dastardly." They may change names, vocabulary, setting, props, and even the ending as it fits their genre. Choose a genre, such as fairy tale, and rewrite the first few lines of the melodrama to reflect the genre. For example:

> **Characters:** *Prince Jocund (the hero), Crystal (the princess), Dragonbreath (the evil wizard), Morgana (a friendly, fire-breathing dragon)*
>
> **Setting:** *A castle far, far away*
>
> **Dragonbreath:** *Ah, my princess, I have cast an evil spell on you! Until you agree to give over all the wealth of your kingdom, you will be trapped in this tower forever!*
>
> **Crystal:** *But all of the peasants will starve! Prince Jocund will save the kingdom!*
>
> *(Dragonbreath lets out a long, evil, bloodcurdling laugh.)*
>
> **Dragonbreath:** *Prince Jocund...well, I have already taken care of him!*

7. Give students plenty of time to rewrite and practice reading and acting out their plays. In this game, groups will be judged on how clearly they represent the genre. All students will fill out a chart, keeping track of vocabulary, situations, settings, and props.

8. Once all teams have performed their plays and filled in their charts, compare the charts. Cluster all of the ideas from the charts under the genre heading on the board. Make sure students understand each genre.

9. Have an awards ceremony and give small prizes to the group that best represented its genre and to the student who filled out the chart most completely.

"Genre Jumble" Elements Chart

52 Engage the Brain: Games • Language Arts, Grades 6–8

Name ____

Directions: Complete this chart about your genre. Use the information to rewrite the melodrama.

Genre: Western

Stock Characters	Settings/Props/ Costumes	Dialect/Vocabulary	Plot Elements
Strong, silent cowboy	Saloon	Howdy, partner!	Good vs. evil
Newcomer in town	Ranch		Save the town
	Desert town		Get rid of villain

Date ____

978-1-4129-5927-8 © Corwin Press

Name _____ Date _____

"Genre Jumble" Elements Chart

Directions: Complete this chart about your genre. Use the information to rewrite the melodrama.

Genre: _____

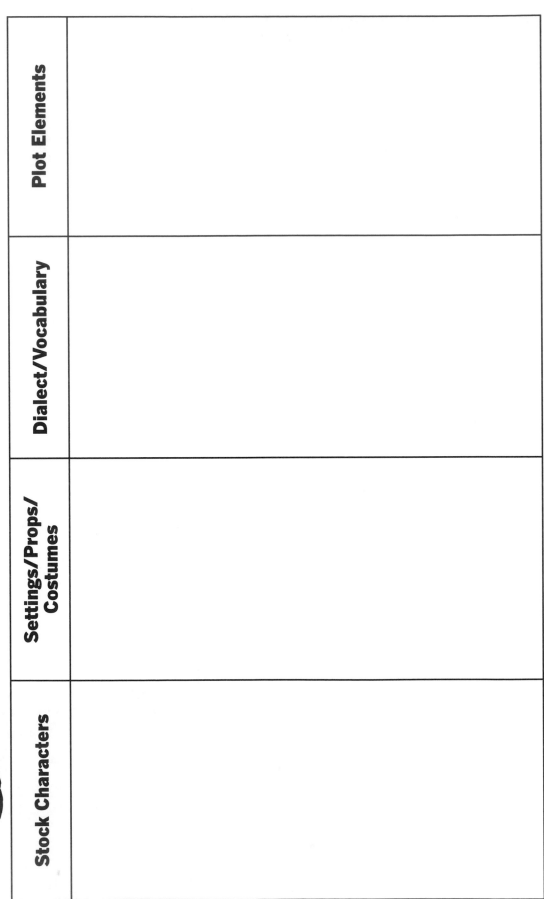

Plot Elements	Dialect/Vocabulary	Settings/Props/Costumes	Stock Characters

Dante the Dastardly

A Melodrama in One Scene

Characters: Dante (the villain), Elizabeth (the damsel in distress), Paolo (the hero)

Setting: A Victorian parlor

(Elizabeth sits working on her embroidery. She wears an old-fashioned long skirt and a blouse. Her hair is pulled up. Music builds. In walks Dante in a black hat and cape. He rubs his hands and twists his mustache. Elizabeth stands, looking afraid.)

Dante: My princess, at long last we are alone! I am here for my answer.

Elizabeth: Ah, Dante! You have been kind to my sick papa. You have rented us a house so that we are not out in the street. But, alas, I cannot marry you!

Dante: Oh, but you can, my sweet. You can!

Elizabeth: I do not love you!

Dante: It is Paolo, isn't it? That baleful brute! He has crept into your heart!

(Dante holds Elizabeth's arm. She attempts to pull away, putting one hand over her brow.)

Dante: Marry me, Elizabeth!

Elizabeth: I cannot!

Dante: *(pulls a paper from his coat)* Then your papa shall pay the price!

Elizabeth: Is this what I think it is? Dante, you wouldn't!

Dante: I would indeed! An eviction—you and your old father shall be on the streets by dinnertime. So what will it be, my little plum blossom? Will you marry rich, handsome, manly me, and forget that fiend Paolo? Or shall your father end his days begging in the snow for scraps? Decide!

(Elizabeth breaks down, sobbing.)

Elizabeth: Alas! Oh my heart is breaking! Paolo ... Papa ... *(she sniffles softly)* What choice have I? What choice but to marry this villain?

Dante the Dastardly (cont.)

(Dante chortles in triumph. Elizabeth weeps.)

Dante: So then, you are mine?

Elizabeth: *(putting a hand to her ear)* What's this? Ah, it is Paolo!

(Paolo bursts in the door.)

Paolo: Elizabeth!

Elizabeth: Paolo!

Dante: She is mine, you wretch! She has agreed to be my wife!

Paolo: It can't be true!

Elizabeth: He will evict Papa! He will throw him into the streets!

(Dante grins and waves the eviction notice proudly.)

Paolo: Give me that!

(They struggle in slow motion over the document. Finally, Paolo wrenches the paper from Dante's grasp.)

Paolo: You will be interested to know, Dante, that I have just been to the Chief of Police! It seems as if you are not Dante after all!

Dante: Lies! Lies!

Paolo: You are a fake! You sent away the real Dante and took his identity! You are Horrible Hank from the Slimy Street Mob, escaped from prison.

Dante: You fool! Now you shall pay the price!

(They brawl in slow motion. Elizabeth breaks a vase over Dante's head. Paolo ties him up. Paolo and Elizabeth embrace.)

Elizabeth: Oh, Paolo! My hero!

Paolo: Elizabeth, will you be my wife?

Elizabeth: Yes, yes, a thousand times yes!

(Last embrace.)

CHAPTER 3

Language Conventions

Sentence Shuffle

Objective

Students will arrange words and punctuation to make logical sentences.

Materials
- Sentence Shuffle reproducible
- Paragraph Shuffle reproducible
- scissors
- envelopes
- timer

Students can never get enough practice in sentence construction. In this game, students will work together to put shuffled sentence parts together in logical order. They will also discuss the purpose and placement of punctuation marks.

1. Tell students that practicing proper sentence structure—the arrangement of words and the use of punctuation—can help them become more effective writers. Write these sentence parts on the board. Ask volunteers how they could arrange the sentence parts to make a logical sentence, including punctuation.

   may be able to travel in space

   and very rich people have the opportunity

   In the future

   for now

   regular citizens

   only astronauts

2. Then write the entire sentence on the board, with the parts put together correctly. Discuss the function of each clause and punctuation mark. Tell students they are going to play a game in which they arrange sentence parts into logical sentences.

   In the future, regular citizens may be able to travel in space; for now, only astronauts and very rich people have the opportunity.

3. Photocopy and cut out the sentence parts on the **Sentence Shuffle reproducible (page 57)**. Place each cut-up sentence into an envelope. Label the envelopes with numbers *1–6*. On each envelope, list the punctuation marks the sentence requires, which is noted on the reproducible.

4. Divide the class into six teams. Give one envelope to each team. Teams must arrange the sentences parts into a sentence that makes sense, and then write the sentence on a piece of paper. As a team, they then add to the sentence the punctuation marks noted on the envelope.

5. After teams are finished, have them exchange envelopes until each team has arranged all six sentences. Ask teams to read aloud their sentences, noting the punctuation marks as they read. The team that makes the least errors wins.

6. Discuss the differences between teams' sentences. Ask students how the sentence changed when certain clauses were in the wrong order or if punctuation was missing. The meaning of the sentence may have changed entirely!

7. Next, invite students to repeat this process using a paragraph. Photocopy and cut out the sentences on the **Paragraph Shuffle reproducible (page 58)**. Make enough sets for six teams. This time, challenge teams to complete the paragraph in a set period of time (e.g., two minutes). Tell students to make sure that the topic sentence is at the beginning and that supporting sentences make logical sense by following the transitions. The first team who finishes their paragraph correctly wins.

Extended Learning
Challenge students to find interesting complex sentences in novels or short stories. Have them write the sentences on strips of paper without punctuation. Then invite students to cut apart the sentences and play Sentence Shuffle with a partner to see who can figure out the sentences first.

978-1-4129-5927-8

Sentence Shuffle

Sentence 1 (2 commas, 1 period)

During the Middle Ages
the plague destroyed one-third
of the population in Europe
and it probably delayed
the discovery of the New World by
approximately 200 years

Sentence 2 (1 comma, 1 semicolon, 1 period)

Fleas carried the disease
from rodents
to people however most
people believed the disease
was a punishment
from God

Sentence 3 (3 commas, 1 period)

People were absolutely
terrified of the disease and
they left
their homes standing empty
their children or parents unburied
and their jobs without notice

Sentence 4 (3 commas, 1 colon, 1 period)

Symptoms of the plague
included the following
purple boils in the
armpits high fever
vomit with blood and finally
death in three days

Sentence 5 (1 comma, 1 period)

Because there were
so few workers
left servants and
serfs were able
to ask for higher
wages and better working conditions

Sentence 6 (6 commas, 1 apostrophe, 1 period)

The plague
also called the Black Death
killed a massive portion
of Europes population
which led to
changes in trade music
art and many other things

ParaGraph Shuffle

One of baseball's favorite legends is that of famous New York Yankee,
Babe Ruth, "calling the shot."

According to the story, the crowds during that third game of the 1932 World Series
were heckling Ruth by throwing lemons and calling him names.

What happened next, some say, is remarkable.

Ruth got up to bat, pointed his finger toward the center field bleachers,
and smacked a home run in the same place he had pointed.

However, according to the pitcher, Charlie Root,
Ruth never pointed at the bleachers before he swung.

Other Chicago Cub team members claimed that Ruth pointed to the players
who were taunting him, not the place where the ball was to land.

Film evidence does indeed show that Babe Ruth pointed before that famous swing,
although it is not clear where he was actually aiming.

Sentence Chains

Objective

Students will work cooperatively to discuss parts of a sentence in order to construct proper complex sentences.

Students will enjoy playing this kinesthetic game, especially when they realize they are playing against the teacher. The following game combines knowledge of phrases and appositives with the creation of unique sentences.

1. Ahead of time, write sentence parts from the **Sentence Chains reproducible (page 61)** on the construction paper strips. Color-coordinate the sentence parts so that all nouns are written on the same-color strips, all verbs are written on the same-color strips, and so on. Enlist student help as needed.

2. Review the parts of a sentence. The core parts of a sentence include the subject (who/what is doing the action) and verb (what the action is). Writers use other sentence parts, such as clauses and phrases, to add color, clarity, description, and detail. In particular, review participial phrases such as *smiling broadly* or *chuckling happily*. These phrases describe in more detail the action that is taking place.

3. Write this sentence on the board: *Travis cried.* This is a complete sentence with a simple subject and verb. Invite the class to add a participial phrase, then an appositive, and then a prepositional phrase. For example, now the sentence might read: *Feeling hungry without his banana, Travis, the monkey with the blue hat, cried into his pink hanky.* Guide students to see how much more colorful and interesting the second sentence is.

4. Give each student three strips with a variety of sentence parts on them. Ask students to write their names on the backs of the strips. Include at least six blank strips so students can add sentence parts, if necessary.

5. Explain to students that they will circulate around the room, finding appropriate sentence parts to chain together. Sentences may (and indeed, should) be complex, but warn students against run-ons and fragments. Point out that the object of the game is for students to work together as a class to create a chain using all three of their sentence parts.

6. Give students a set amount of time to find and chain up all their sentence parts (they can use tape, glue, or staplers). The class will begin with 100 points. They will lose:
   - one point for each sentence part not used
   - two points for every sentence part incorrectly used
   - three points for mistakes in structure (e.g., fragments, run-ons)
   - five points for sentences that make no sense

7. Provide some kind of simple reward or incentive for the class to win, such as a homework pass or a special snack. If the class can keep 90 out of 100 points, they win!

8. Close the game by asking students to break down several sentence chains into subjects and predicates.

Extended Learning

Have students write a short story or paragraph based on their silliest sentences. Remind them to use these sentence parts in their own writing to add complexity and interest to stories and essays.

Sentence Chains

SUBJECTS OR OBJECTS

the lonely giraffe
the white whale
the vicious tornado
the stealthy vampire
Sheba, the warrior princess,
the wicked English teacher
the entire class
the old, decrepit cowboy
the team of astronauts
Ricardo, the super chef,
the germ infestation
the plague of rabid rodents
the jubilant soccer team
the excited salsa dancer
the heat of the day

VERBS

whined
celebrated
were
was
danced
frightened
served
scratched
baked
sobbed
fought
sneaked
felt
destroyed
crept

PREPOSITIONAL PHRASES

in the brush
along Broadway

into the night
on the island
by breakfast time
against each other
with friends
without a clue
under a bridge
in a treasure chest
by the cactus
beneath a palm tree
into the castle
in the crowded stands
in a pink boa

CONJUNCTIONS

and
and
and
but
but
except

PARTICIPIAL PHRASES

wearing a red suit
feeling haughty
squealing with fright
protesting violently
smiling broadly
chuckling evilly
sighing sadly
boasting proudly
giggling uncontrollably
showing off their muscles
tapping their toes
snoring heartily
feeling happy and in love
creeping quietly

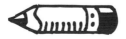    

Five Alive! Bingo

Objective

Students will review a wide variety of grammar, figurative language, and literary terms as they play a game.

This game is an old favorite made new. Played in the style of Bingo, students make their own game boards and compete to get five in a row—Five Alive! To play successfully, students will need to show their knowledge of grammar, figurative language, and literary devices.

1. Have students name some of the favorite games they played when they were younger. Explain that they will play an "amped up" version of Bingo. It will test their knowledge of grammar, figurative language, and literary terms they have learned.

2. Display a transparency of the **Five Alive! Bingo Categories reproducible (page 64)** on the overhead projector, and review the list with students. (Ahead of time, add any of your own categories to the end of the list (numbers *30–36*). Review some of the more difficult terms, such as *onomatopoeia, homonym, root word, type of clause or phrase*, or *literary genre*.

3. Give students a copy of the **Five Alive! Bingo Game Board reproducible (page 65)**. Tell them that before they play the game, they will make their own game boards. Have students fill in the game board in any order using categories from the list, one category for each box. They may repeat any categories they wish on the same game board.

4. Next, have students count off, one at a time, from *1* to *36*. Keeping the Five Alive! Bingo Categories reproducible displayed, ask students to write at least three examples for their assigned categories. These will be called out during the game, similar to how numbers are called out during Bingo. For example, student number *1* will write nouns that are people (e.g., *baby, uncle, firefighter*). Have students carefully rip or cut out their examples, fold them, and then place them in a paper bag. Make sure each student has provided at least three examples for the game.

5. Review the game rules with students, and then begin the game. Draw a category from the bag, and call out one example at a time as students mark squares on their game boards. For example, if you call out *Harry Potter*, students place a game marker on the square labeled *character in novel* or *proper noun*.

6. The first person to get five in a row (up and down, across, or diagonal) shouts: *Five Alive!*

7. After the game, check for understanding by calling out categories from the reproducible and asking volunteers to provide examples.

Extended Learning

As you learn new concepts in class, add them to your category sheet. By the end of the year, play the game again to show students how much they have learned!

noun (thing)	proper noun (place)	noun (person)	action verb	literary device
title of short story	title of poem	title of novel	famous author	tone word
type of poem	setting	famous author	root word	noun (idea)
literary device	adverb	noun (thing)		

Five Alive! Bingo Categories

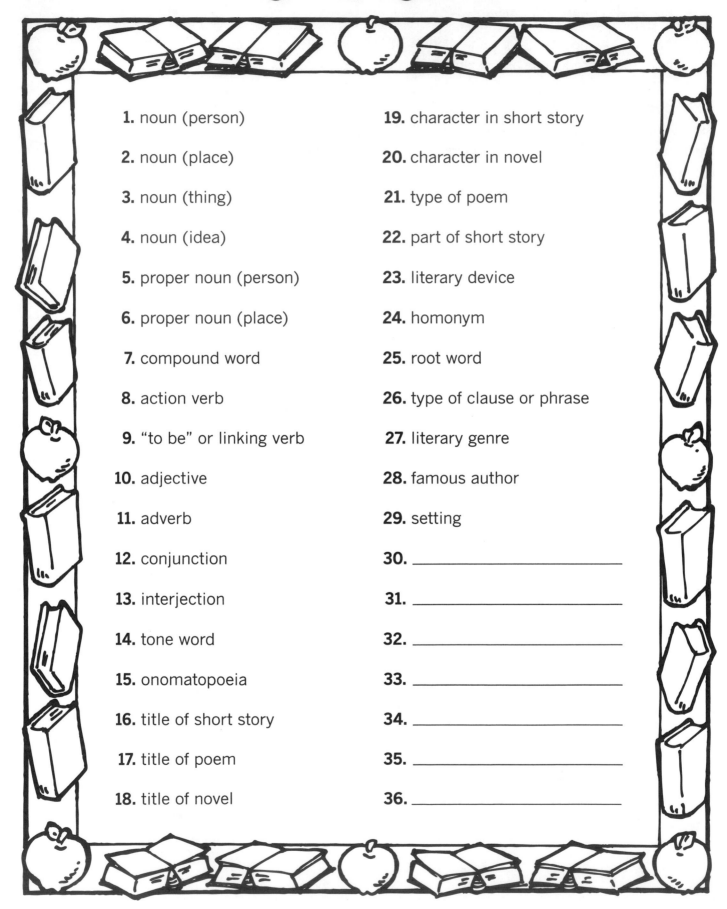

1. noun (person)
2. noun (place)
3. noun (thing)
4. noun (idea)
5. proper noun (person)
6. proper noun (place)
7. compound word
8. action verb
9. "to be" or linking verb
10. adjective
11. adverb
12. conjunction
13. interjection
14. tone word
15. onomatopoeia
16. title of short story
17. title of poem
18. title of novel

19. character in short story
20. character in novel
21. type of poem
22. part of short story
23. literary device
24. homonym
25. root word
26. type of clause or phrase
27. literary genre
28. famous author
29. setting
30. _____
31. _____
32. _____
33. _____
34. _____
35. _____
36. _____

Name _____ Date _____

Five Alive! Bingo Game Board

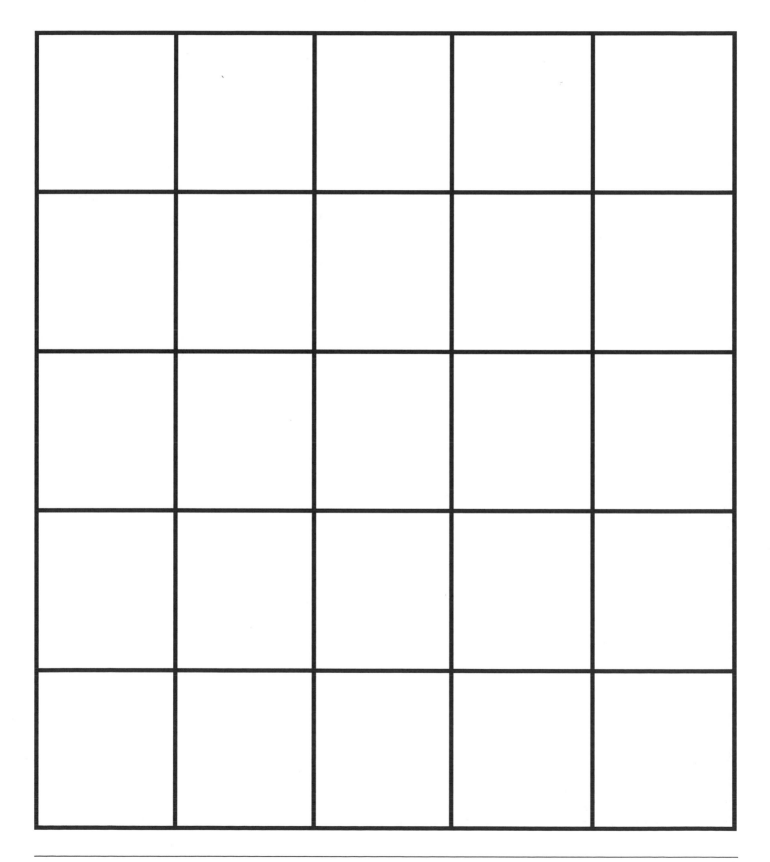

Cap It! Relay

Objective
Students will review capitalization rules.

In this activity, students will race to correct capitalization in sentences. Students will have to move quickly to win this game!

1. Some capitalization rules come naturally. Ask students for examples such as beginnings of sentences or names of people and states. Other rules are less familiar, such as capitalizing certain government terms and names of ships. This game is an effective way to reinforce the variety of capitalization rules.

2. Copy each sentence from the **Cap It! Relay Sentences reproducibles (pages 68–69)** onto two butcher paper strips, large enough for students to see. Display one sentence at a time on opposite walls, so that each team will be working with the same sentence.

3. Divide the class into six teams, and give each team copies of the Cap It! Relay Sentences reproducibles cut into sentence strips and a pad of sticky notes. Tell students not to touch the strips until you say so. Have each team choose a "runner"—one who will run to the butcher paper and make corrections.

4. Explain the rules of the game:
   a. At your signal, teams must find the sentence strip that matches the one displayed.
   b. Team members must work together to decide which words in the sentence need to be capitalized, writing directly on their sentence strip.
   c. One team member writes the correct capital letters for each word, one per sticky note.
   d. The first two teams to finish send their runners with the corrected sentence strip and sticky notes to the butcher paper sentence. Runners stick the capital letters to the words as fast as possible to beat the other team.
   e. Once two teams have reached both of the butcher paper sentences, the other four teams must wait to play until the next round. (Note: Teams who go to the butcher paper without their original sentence strip and the finished sticky notes are automatically disqualified for that round.)

f. The team who correctly finishes first receives ten points; however, make sure to go over finished work, asking the other teams to check for errors. If the other team is also correct, they receive five points.

g. After each round, ask each team why the correct capital letter is necessary and to explain the capitalization rule. Teams get one point for each correct response.

h. The team with the most points after ten sentences wins the game!

5. After the game, invite students to share the mistakes they made. Go back over the rules for the words that must be capitalized and those that should not. Later in the week, play the game again using different sentences (or ask students to write them). See how well students remember the capitalization rules.

Extended Learning

After the game, distribute copies of the Cap It! Relay Sentences reproducibles. Challenge students to correct each sentence individually to see how much they learned from the game.

In April 1912, the Titanic sailed from Southampton, England, to Cherbourg, France.

Cap It! Relay Sentences

1. in april 1912, the *titanic* sailed from southampton, england, to cherbourg, france, and finally to queenstown, ireland, to pick up the many millionaires who were to board the ship.

2. colonel john jacob aster, famous for owning real estate in manhattan, including the famous waldorf astoria hotel, sailed with his dog kitty and was among the most famous first-class travelers on the *titanic*.

3. isidor straus, who served as a u.s. congressman and was a mentor to grover cleveland, was another millionaire who made his fortune in new york city. he started a glassware business in the corner of macy's department store.

4. isidor's wife ida refused to leave her husband and stayed aboard the *titanic* on that fateful saturday night. she then gave her fur coat to her maid stating, "it will be cold in the lifeboat."

5. harry widener had traveled to europe to add to his book collection and had purchased a rare edition of a book by sir francis bacon; however, neither he nor his text survived.

6. benjamin guggenheim, a swiss american, stands out from the other millionaires aboard the white star line ship. he changed into his formal evening clothes before the *titanic* sank, apparently so he could die looking like a gentleman.

7. margaret brown, otherwise known as the "unsinkable molly brown," had met new york's elite couple, j. j. astor and his wife madeleine, on an egyptian vacation.

8. when molly brown's husband heard she had survived the *titanic*, he exclaimed, "she's too mean to sink!"

9. guglielmo marconi, another passenger, invented the wireless telegraph that was used to call out the s.o.s. signals to the rescuing ship, the *carpathia*.

10. the *titanic* hit an iceberg in the north atlantic sea approximately 400 miles from newfoundland. many of the millionaire travelers were saved, while virtually none of the third-class passengers lived.

Paper Plate Stomp

Materials
- Word List: Level 1 reproducible
- Word List: Level 2 reproducible
- 60+ paper plates
- markers
- whistle

Objective
Students will review parts of speech through physical movement.

Some learners especially excel during kinesthetic learning activities. This game is another version of tag, which allows students to move around and make some noise while reviewing the parts of speech.

1. Ahead of time, review the **Word List: Level 1** and **Word List: Level 2 reproducibles (pages 72–73)** to determine which level (or combination of the two) is more appropriate for your class.

2. Use markers to write your word list on paper plates, one word per plate, in big, bold print. Write parts of speech that show only a few words (such as articles) several times.

3. Write the following sentence on the board: *"Ouch! Your sharp, shiny braces cut my lip!" the frog exclaimed rudely to Princess Amelia.* Invite students to break the sentence apart by naming the speech parts, including articles, nouns, verbs, pronouns, adjectives, adverbs, conjunctions, prepositions, and interjections.

4. Tell students that they are going to play a game to review the parts of speech. Then take them outside to a large playing area, or have them help you move all the desks against the walls so you can play in the middle of the classroom. Place the paper plates on the ground, spaced widely apart.

5. Then explain how to play the game:
   a. You will call out the parts of speech, one at a time.
   b. Students must place a foot on a plate with a word matching that part of speech. For example, if you call out *adjective*, students must find words that are adjectives, such as *gorgeous* or *smelly*. Blow a whistle after a few moments; students must "freeze" in place on their paper plates.
   c. You will tap on the shoulder of all students who chose an incorrect word (that doesn't match the part of speech called out). These students must sit out the rest of the game.
   d. The winner or winners are those who remain standing, correctly matching all parts of speech to the correct words.

6. Ask a couple of volunteers to help model one or two rounds of the game so students understand how to play. Then begin the game. After several students are out, you may invite one or two of them to help you call out parts of speech.

7. After the game, encourage students to write on the board the words that got them "out." Review those words, making sure students understand their function in a sentence.

Extended Learning

For a second round of Paper Plate Stomp, divide the class into two teams and separate the paper plates into two piles, one pile per team. The team who can write the longest complete sentence using their words wins round two! After sentences are complete, invite students to recite the part of speech for each word. For example, if students create the sentence: *The silly snake immediately cut his stinky steak after sunset,* they would say: *article, adjective, noun, adverb, verb, pronoun, adjective, noun, preposition, noun.*

Word List: Level 1

ARTICLES

a
an
the

NOUNS

adventure
aunt
farm
king
planet
pumpkin
snake
steak
sunset
tornado

VERBS

believe
cut
decide
is
scratch
scream
speak
stretch
yawn
yearn

PRONOUNS

he
her
his
I
my
our
she
their
you

ADJECTIVES

annoying
crusty
dusty
evil
frozen
gorgeous
purple
silly
slimy
stinky

INTERJECTIONS

darn!
oh!
oops!
ouch!
uh oh!
well!
wow!
yeah!

CONJUNCTIONS

and
but
for
nor
or
yet

PREPOSITIONS

about
across
after
between
by
during
through
to
under
within

ADVERBS

angrily
far
gladly
hungrily
immediately
quietly
scarcely
there
usually
very

Word List: Level 2

RELATIVE PRONOUNS

that
which
who
whom
whose

INTERROGATIVE PRONOUNS

what
which
who
whom
whose

DEMONSTRATIVE PRONOUNS

that
these
this
those

INDEFINITE PRONOUNS

all
another
any
each
either
more
none
one
other

PROPER NOUNS

America
Flicks Movie Theater
Harvard University
King Arthur
January
Monday
Mrs. Garcia
Texas

COMPOUND NOUNS

commander in chief
cowboy
drugstore
firefighter
housekeeper
marketplace
merry-go-round
mother-in-law
police officer
spaceship

LINKING VERBS

appear
be
become
feel
grow
look
remain
sound

ABSTRACT NOUNS

delight
devotion
disgust
freedom
happiness
jealousy
joy
love
perfection
sophistication
wisdom

Grammar Charades

Materials
- Grammar Charades Word List reproducible
- scissors
- hat or bowl
- timer

Objective
Students will mime words and earn points according to their knowledge of the parts of speech.

Many students love acting and others love playing games. This activity combines both. Students must know their parts of speech in order to succeed in this take on traditional charades.

1. Ahead of time, cut out the words on the **Grammar Charades Word List reproducible (page 76)** and place them in a hat or bowl.

2. Review the parts of speech with students. Write the following in one line across the board: *Article / adjective / compound noun / verb / conjunction / verb / adverb / preposition / article / noun. Interjection!* As a class, come up with a sentence that fits this pattern. For example, *The fluorescent flying saucer hovered and tilted wildly among the stars. Yikes!* Make sure students recall the parts of speech. Invite them to write and then share sentences that fit this format.

3. Divide the class into four teams and call forward one student from each team. Explain that each team begins with 20 points. Write the point scale on the board:
   - *Three or fewer guesses: ten points*
   - *Four to six guesses: five points*
   - *Seven to ten guesses: two points*

4. Flip a coin to see which team begins. The first player pulls a word from the hat, silently reads the word, and gives the part of speech (e.g., *noun, verb*). If that player cannot identify the part of speech, he or she must pass the turn to a teammate. He or she then acts out the word. The team gets one minute to guess the word that is being acted out. The player cannot speak, only gesture.

5. Instead of shouting out guesses, team members must guess one at a time. Explain that students must guess in an ordered fashion, with each team member getting a turn. If the team cannot guess the word, allow the next team to guess.

6. Players can lose points for guessing incorrect parts of speech. For example, if the player chooses the word *boomerang* and states that the word is a common noun, a team member who guesses *throw* will have a point subtracted because *throw* is a verb rather than a common noun.

7. Model the game for students by pulling a word from the hat and saying the part of speech. Then act out the word for the class. Remind students to guess one at a time. When you are sure students understand the directions, let them begin. During the game, you will be the scorekeeper. Ask a volunteer to time each team as they take their turns.

8. To close the activity, invite students to make their own word lists for more rounds of Grammar Charades. This will reinforce their knowledge of the parts of speech.

Grammar Charades Word List

Common Nouns	Verbs	Proper Nouns	Adverbs
glove	argue	King Kong	happily
coffee	destroy	Statue of Liberty	carefully
kitten	admire	Prince Charming	nervously
ocean	waltz	William Shakespeare	hungrily
tornado	forgive	Africa	sweetly
jungle	annoy	Los Angeles Lakers	noisily
soldier	adore	King Arthur	hurriedly
egg	weep	George Washington	sleepily
leaf	leap	Australia	proudly

Compound Nouns	Adjectives	Prepositions	Interjections
hairspray	flirtatious	around	Oh no!
flying saucer	bizarre	beneath	Ouch!
baseball bat	hideous	between	No!
compact disc	crazy	among	Eek!
steering wheel	shocking	under	Hurray!
merry-go-round	sour	by	Darn!
jack-o-lantern	adorable	outside	Wow!
lunch box	cozy	beyond	Aha!
ball and chain	greedy	over	Yum!

Error Bearers

Objective

Students will edit sentences for a variety of mechanical errors.

Materials
- Error Bearers reproducible
- index cards
- marker
- overhead projector and transparency

It can be a challenge to get students to look closely at the rules and reasons for language conventions. In this competition, they must analyze, discuss, and remember their grammar and mechanics rules.

1. Ahead of time, prepare number cards for the game. Write the numbers *1–5* (one number on each index card) in bold marker for each set. Prepare six or more sets.

2. Tell students that getting into the habit of checking for common errors can ease the writing process. Invite students to think of other things they automatically double-check (e.g., bike locks, hair and teeth, correctly spelled e-mail addresses). Explain that this game will help them get into the habit of double-checking for writing errors.

3. Copy the **Error Bearers reproducible (page 79)** onto a transparency or PowerPoint® slides. Then display some common errors students made in a previous writing assignment. Review how to correct the errors. Tell students that this game will cover many types of errors that are often found in their writing.

4. Divide the class into teams of three to five. Give each team a set of five index cards (numbered *1–5*). Give each team a name or number. Assign a scorekeeper at the board. Then explain how to play the game:
   a. All players read and review displayed sentences. In teams, they must identify and discuss the errors and then total the number of errors. They must decide how many errors each sentence "bears."
   b. Players have a minute or so to discuss and decide on the answer. They must be ready with the card that indicates the number of errors. On a count of three, all teams must raise their number cards.
   c. Teams with the correct number of errors get one point, and the scorekeeper records the scores. He or she will use the following answer key for reference:

Answer Key

1.	five errors	7.	three errors
2.	three errors	8.	four errors
3.	three errors	9.	two errors
4.	two errors	10.	three errors
5.	five errors	11.	four errors
6.	three errors	12.	one error

5. Model for students by writing two or three sentences on the board. Make sure each sentence contains one to five errors each. Ask the class to examine the first sentence and determine the number of errors. After a minute, have them hold up their number cards. Repeat with the remaining sentences until students understand and are comfortable with the process.

6. Then invite students to play the game. Display the sentences one at a time, and give teams about one minute to determine the number of errors before holding up their number cards.

7. After the game, give students a copy of the Error Bearers reproducible. Have them correct the errors on the reproducible and discuss their corrections.

Extended Learning

Have students look through their writing portfolio to search for errors in their writing. Ask them to rewrite these sentences, correcting the errors as they go. Then have students use their own error-bearing sentences for another round of the game.

978-1-4129-5927-8

Error Bearers

1. In medieval times the Standard of Beauty was different than todays.

2. Woman whom had large foreheads and clear skin were considered more attractive?

3. Some ladys plucked out the hair around they're foreheads to make it look larger.

4. Many women liked men who where heavy because they believed they was rich, and could afford to eat.

5. A huge part of the population had small pox many people had scars on there faces so those who excaped the disease was lucky.

6. midevil society also admired people who had all of their teeth, because many lost teeth do to decay, a lack of toothbrushes, and the ignorance of dentist's.

7. Onions and garlic was the most popular vegetables therefore people's breath smell unpleasant.

8. Because people believe that dirt on skin kept away diseases. Most pesants took baths only once a year

9. There was no such thing as deodorant soap was made of fat.

10. Yuck people who lived during this time period, cleaned their garments with lard.

11. In The Canterbury Tales a book by Geoffrey Chaucer a woman was considered beautiful if she has gapped teeth.

12. Are'nt you glad you didn't live back then?

Word Power

Objective

Students will compete to brainstorm words that match certain parts of speech.

One of the best strategies students can use to remember important information is to play games. In this engaging game, students will stretch their minds to brainstorm various parts of speech that begin with specific letters.

1. Review the parts of speech with students. Ask volunteers to provide you with several examples of each kind of word. Prompt them to explain the meaning of each part of speech and how it helps build a sentence or make it more interesting.

2. Write a part of speech in large letters across the board, such as *adverb*.

3. Tell students that they will compete to see how many adverbs they can think of beginning with each letter of the word. See the following example.

A	D	V	E	R	B
angrily	daringly	very	eerily	rarely	brightly
	desperately	~~vast~~		roughly	barely

4. Have students write *adverb* horizontally across their own paper and then work with a partner or trio. Set a timer for three minutes, and have teams write as many words as they can.

5. After the timer sounds, ask teams to count the number of adverbs on their papers.

6. Invite students to raise their hands as you count upward. For example: *How many teams have 10 or more? 15 or more?* and so on. Ask the top three winners to switch papers with each other.

7. Ask each of the three winners to read the answers aloud and point out any that are not adverbs. In the example, *vast* is not an adverb; it is an adjective. This word would be crossed off the list. This part of the game is crucial for refining and retaining learning.

8. The team with the most correct answers wins that round. Next, move on to adjective, noun, preposition, and so on.

9. Invite students to keep their word lists in their writing folders for future reference when writing essays, reports, or stories.

Extended Learning

Use this game for teaching parts of a sentence, such as prepositional phrase, gerund, appositive, and participial phrase. Ask students to work in pairs to write sentences starting with the appropriate letters and define the sentence part.

The example below uses the sentence part *participle*:

Putting the dishes away, Santiago cut his finger.

Arguing and whining, Alyssa eventually got her way.

Reading carefully, Thao figured out most of the questions.

Tired and hassled, the teacher finally gave up.

Icing the cupcakes, I planned out the party games.

Cracked and scratched, the plate was worthless.

Interested in nothing, Brianne sat pouting in the corner.

Primping and smiling in the mirror, Hitesh liked what he saw.

Lapping hungrily, the kitten licked the bowl clean.

Eyeing the steaming apple pie, Jenny moved hungrily toward the table.

CHAPTER 4

Listening and Speaking

Lingo Ladder

Materials
- Lingo Ladder Category Cards reproducibles
- scissors
- construction paper
- markers
- timer

Objective
Students will learn about dialect and colloquialisms while playing a game based on the TV show *$10,000 Pyramid*.

In this game, students have the opportunity to discuss dialect and local color. While working with clues and categories, students will practice speaking and listening skills.

1. Define and discuss the terms *dialect* and *local color*. *Dialect* is the language of a particular group of people. It includes pronunciation, word choice, and spelling, and shows social and geographic characteristics. *Local color* is a literary term used to describe the flavor, interests, and customs of a particular group.

2. Ask students to describe their own dialect and local color. For example, ask them to share phrases they use when speaking with friends. Ask students: *How do you like to dress? What do you do for fun?* Offer descriptions of dialect and social customs of different groups of people in the community. Allow students to contribute descriptions. Be sure to guide conversation toward neutral or positive observations about different groups.

3. Divide the class into teams of five. Give each team one card from the **Lingo Ladder Category Cards reproducibles (pages 84–85)**. Have each team pull their desks together and quietly come up with clues for their categories. For example, for the category *Words a surfer would use to describe the beach*, clues might include: *gnarly, awesome, tubular, offshore, pipeline*. (The word *surf* cannot be a clue.) Urge teams to come up with as many clues as possible for each category. Clues should be four words or less.

4. Next, have each team write each of its six categories on a separate sheet of construction paper. Ask them to rank the categories from easiest to most difficult. They will label the easiest three as *100* points, the next two as *200* points, and the most difficult as *300* points. Make sure students write the points on the back of the construction paper in large, bold letters.

978-1-4129-5927-8

5. Collect all student papers, and check students' clues for accuracy. Then tape the papers to a wall with the points showing. Place a 300-point clue at the top, two 200-point clues in the middle, and three 100-point clues at the bottom.

6. Pair up teams with each other, and explain that they will be working together to earn points. One team will face the other in front of the class. Starting with the 100-point categories, one team gives clues and the other team tries to guess the category. Direct team members to take turns giving clues and taking guesses. They will have three minutes to give clues for the category. If they fail to guess the category in three minutes, they must move on to the next one. Both teams will receive the point total for correct answers. Teams then switch roles for the next category until all categories in the pyramid are used.

300

200   200

100   Words or phrases toddlers would use when they are sleepy   Words or phrases a professional athlete would use

7. Before letting students begin, ask a couple of volunteers to work through one of the categories with you. Give clues to students and have them take turns taking guesses. Make sure they understand to work with 100-point categories first and work their way up.

8. Invite students to begin the game while you keep track of time and points. After one round, the next two teams play. The team with the most points wins!

9. After the game, initiate a class discussion about the clues used. Prompt students with questions such as: *What other clues would have helped you guess the categories more quickly? Were clues specific enough or too vague?*

Extended Learning

Brainstorm the dialect of other groups who have specific vocabulary. Ask students to write a paragraph using dialect and local color, without identifying the group. Have students switch papers and try to guess the group being described.

Lingo Ladder Category Cards

Category 1: Words or phrases a surfer would use to describe the beach

Category 2: Words or phrases that may have been used to get women the right to vote

Category 3: Words or phrases an elderly person would use to describe your school

Category 4: Words or phrases an alien would use

Category 5: Words or phrases a vegetarian would use at a fast food restaurant

Category 6: Words or phrases a farmer would use

Category 1: Words or phrases a scientist would use to describe an attractive woman

Category 2: Words or phrases toddlers would use when they are sleepy

Category 3: Words or phrases a lovesick man would use to get a date with his beloved

Category 4: Words or phrases someone participating in Martin Luther King Jr.'s sit-ins would use

Category 5: Words or phrases a professional athlete would use

Category 6: Words or phrases uptight parents would use when they saw their child's messy room

---

Category 1: Words or phrases a used car salesman would use

Category 2: Words or phrases young girls would shout out to their favorite singer or band

Category 3: Words or phrases cavemen or cavewomen would use upon seeing your city

Category 4: Words or phrases an angry teacher would use after a spitball fight

Category 5: Words or phrases a computer technician would use

Category 6: Words or phrases a very polite southern belle would use to decline a date

Lingo Ladder Category Cards

Category 1: Words or phrases someone signing the Declaration of Independence would use

Category 2: Words or phrases a vampire would use

Category 3: Words or phrases children would use when their parents refuse to buy them something they want

Category 4: Words or phrases the queen of England would use

Category 5: Words or phrases a beauty pageant winner would use

Category 6: Words or phrases this movie/television star would use: _____

Category 1: Words or phrases cheerleaders would use to sell candy for their team

Category 2: Words or phrases a knight in the Middle Ages would use

Category 3: Words or phrases someone who loves math would use

Category 4: Words or phrases someone conducting a serious news interview would use

Category 5: Words or phrases an aerobics instructor would use to motivate a class

Category 6: Words or phrases a dentist would use

Category 1: Words or phrases a dog groomer would use

Category 2: Words or phrases a lawyer would use in a court case

Category 3: Words or phrases Prince Charming would *really* use

Category 4: Words or phrases the richest people in the world would use

Category 5: Words or phrases a clown at a child's party would use

Category 6: Words or phrases Shakespeare would use

It's Like This!

Materials
- It's Like This! Topics List reproducible
- scissors
- bag or box
- timer

Objective
Students will practice thinking and speaking quickly as they review metaphors and similes.

Students should already be familiar with similes and metaphors, but they may still struggle with using them effectively. In this fast-thinking game of figurative language and poetry, students pull words out of a box and quickly create unusual comparisons before time is up.

1. Write the following sentence on the board: *Look like the innocent flower, but be the serpent under it.* Ask students: *What does this phrase mean?* Explain that Lady Macbeth speaks this line in Shakespeare's play, *Macbeth*. In this line, Lady Macbeth uses both simile and metaphor—she tells Macbeth to look innocent *like a flower*, but to *be a serpent* (have evil intent) underneath.

2. Review similes and metaphors—they compare one thing to something completely different. Similes use the words *like* or *as* in the comparison, whereas metaphors do not.

3. Ask students to think of other similes and metaphors. Then write these sentence frames on the board, and invite students to help you complete them:
   Lady Macbeth is like a _____ because _____. (simile)
   Our school is like a _____ because _____. (simile)
   The screaming baby was a _____ to my ears. (metaphor)

4. Divide the class into four teams. Give each team a different topic from the first column below.

Metaphor and Simile Topics

true love	winter	homework	grief
death	spring	chores	joy
breaking up	summer	waking up	hate
growing up	fall	the weekend	forgiveness

5. Cut out the words from the **It's Like This! Topics List reproducible (page 88)**, and place them in a bag or box. Then explain how to play the game:
   a. The first team lines up in front of a row of chairs. One at a time, players draw a word from the box.
   b. Each player must create a metaphor or simile comparing that word to his or her topic. For example, the first player

draws the word *snake*. He or she has 45 seconds to create a metaphor or simile comparing *true love* to a *snake*. The comparison must make sense and show *how* or *why* the topic is like the word.

    c. If the player cannot answer in 45 seconds, he or she must sit down. The next player in line may take the same word or choose a new one.

    d. After a player gives an acceptable answer, the class must decide whether it is a simile or a metaphor.

    e. Tally one point for every acceptable simile or metaphor.

    f. Once all team members are sitting, the next team gets a turn.

    g. Play continues for several rounds. The team with the most points wins!

6. Practice a few examples together before you begin. Using *snake* and *true love*, an acceptable answer might be: *True love is like a snake that squeezes your heart so tight you feel dizzy* (simile), or *True love is a snake, wrapping around you until you can barely breathe* (metaphor). An unacceptable answer might be: *True love is a cold snake.*

7. Invite students to play the game. After all four teams are finished with round one, try a second round with topics from a classroom literature selection or those listed on page 86.

8. After the game, invite students to share which topics and words were the most difficult to compare. List them on the board. Together, brainstorm different ways to compare the two, using both similes and metaphors. Inspire creativity!

Extended Learning

Have students go on a "scavenger hunt" to find interesting metaphors and similes. They can search graphic novels, commercials, magazines, cartoons, and classroom reading to find new comparisons. Hang a long piece of butcher paper on your door and encourage students to record their findings for the class.

It's Like This! Topics List

snake	poison	tornado	kitten
gravestone	monster	river	mountain
spaghetti	steak	rainstorm	lightning
seashell	ocean	tidal wave	tree
high-heeled shoe	flannel pajamas	window	vampire
soda	fountain	cup of coffee	lipstick
video game	skateboard	alien	reality TV show
football	sunshine	box of crayons	spider
fish	hamster	cactus	star
bag of chips	princess	perfume	mold
eagle	mosquito	daisy	candy
chewed gum	castle	gargoyle	baseball bat
rodeo	clown	race car	orange peel
camera	broken mirror	raisin	Big Foot
tutu	flamingo	wind	microphone
fire	ghost	angel	carnival
cannibal	bumblebee	flag	knife
monkey	scuba diver	sickness	skeleton
cupcake	computer	kiss	hug

Forbidden Phrases

Objective

Students will earn points by describing literary concepts and characters in precise and creative ways.

Materials
- index cards (or squares of construction paper)
- markers
- bells or other noisemakers
- timer

Students almost always respond to challenges by rising to the occasion. In this game, played similarly to the popular commercial game *Taboo®* (a registered trademark of Hersch and Company), students will be challenged to think of precise, inventive, and creative language to describe literature topics. Teams will review concepts as they both create and play this game.

1. Tell the class they will create and play a game similar to Taboo®. Ask students who have played the game to share the rules with the rest of the class. Explain that they will first create the game before they play it.

2. Show students an example of a card they will create for the game. Draw a card on the board. Write the name of a character from literature you've read in class. For example, write *Little Ann* from *Where the Red Fern Grows* on the "card." Ask students to think of five important words they would use to describe Little Ann. For example, *dog/hound, Old Dan, Billy, coon, hunt.* Write these on the board.

3. Model the upcoming game by asking a volunteer to describe Little Ann without using the words on the board. He or she will have to think of other descriptors, ideas, or events in the life of Little Ann that classmates will understand and be able to use to identify the character.

4. Tell the class they will create cards like this to play Forbidden Phrases. As a class, brainstorm examples of characters, themes, places, and actions from a class literature selection. For each category (e.g., character, theme), list six ideas. For example, in *Where the Red Fern Grows*, the "character" category might include: *Billy Coleman, Old Dan, Little Ann, Papa, Grandfather, Mama,* and *Billy's sisters.*

5. Divide the class into teams of six. Give each team six index cards and assign a category from the board. Students will write one entry on each card and then underneath, write the five most obvious descriptors.

For example:

6. Tell teams to switch cards with another team. Have each team break into two teams of three. Then explain how to play the game:
   a. The first team of three to play chooses someone to read the first card. The player gives the category only (e.g., *character*).
   b. That player then has 45 seconds to give clues to his or her teammates so they can guess the specific character. The player cannot use any of the words listed on the card.
   c. A member of the opposing team monitors play and rings a bell or other noisemaker (like a kazoo) if the player uses a word on the card. If one of those words is used, that team loses a turn.
   d. Continue playing several rounds, making sure each student gets a chance to play. Teams receive one point for every correct guess.
   e. At the end of a set number of rounds, the team with the most points wins!

7. After the game, invite students to discuss the clues they used to successfully communicate the topics. Have them record these ideas in their writing journals for future reference.

Extended Learning

Give each student a card from the game. Ask students to write a paragraph explaining the topic without using any of the clues listed. They will need to really stretch their vocabularies and descriptions. Allow time for students to read their paragraphs aloud, so the class can guess the topics.

Media Mix

Objective

Students will question, challenge, or confirm commercials in a game that requires quick thinking and media evaluation.

Materials
- videotaped commercials
- baton or beanbag
- timer

The media bombards students every day with music, television shows, magazine articles, and especially, advertising. In this game, students watch commercials and work quickly to evaluate them and then develop questions, challenges, or confirmations of products.

1. Initiate a class discussion about commercials and advertising. Prompt students with questions such as: *How do commercials influence you? Which commercials affect you the most? Why? How does the media get us to believe in certain products? What strategies and tricks do they use?*

2. Explain that we must pay attention to things we hear on television and the radio. It is an advertiser's job to make us want something that we might not have wanted before. A good method of analyzing commercials is to question, challenge, or confirm an advertiser's claims.

3. Discuss the three strategies for analyzing media: *question, challenge,* and *confirm*. We can *question* why advertisers choose particular music, actors, settings, and scripts. We can *challenge* a media claim by demanding an explanation or justification for the claim. We can *confirm* an idea by agreeing with it based on given facts, evidence, or personal experience.

4. Show a commercial to the class. Ask students to watch it carefully, looking for techniques to influence the audience, including vague words, name calling, or specific settings and actors. Urge students to think of questions, challenges, or confirmations for what the commercial is trying to sell. Provide some examples for students based on the commercial.

5. Write these three phrases on the board, and then tell students that they will play a game that helps them evaluate and analyze advertisements.
   - *I question*
   - *I challenge*
   - *I confirm*

6. Break the class into four teams. Then explain how to play the game:
   a. One team comes to the front of the room and stands in a line.
   b. The first player holds a baton or beanbag.
   c. The class views a commercial, and each player has one minute to think of a question, a challenge, or a confirmation about what the commercial is promoting.
   d. The first player gives an answer, and then passes the baton to the next player in line.
   e. If that player cannot come up with an acceptable question, challenge, or confirmation in one minute, he or she must sit down. The last player standing wins that round.
   f. The winners from the four teams play one final playoff round to determine the last one standing!

7. Play a new commercial for each round. You can judge students' answers on your own, or invite a "panel" of judges made up of student volunteers.

8. After the game, discuss the four commercials. Recall interesting questions or challenges students contributed. Ask which commercials they found most effective and why.

Extended Learning
- For homework, have students watch a segment of the news. Ask them to think of and write at least two questions, challenges, and confirmations about the news stories. Invite students to share their findings with the class.

- Suggest that students evaluate other forms of media, including print and radio ads. Post print ads around the room and have students walk around, view the ads, and write questions, challenges, and confirmations.

 978-1-4129-5927-8

Sinking Ship

Objective

Students will practice spelling, defining, and using vocabulary in context in a game of speedy speech.

Materials
- vocabulary or spelling word list
- timer
- small squares of paper or index cards (cut in half)

Here's a twist on flashcards and rote memorization for vocabulary or spelling practice. In this game, teams will work together in order to stay "afloat"! This activity works well for reviewing any set of vocabulary or spelling words.

1. To pique students' interest, say aloud a word they mostly likely will not know (e.g., *deluge*). Explain that in order to use this word easily and comfortably, students will need to know how to spell it, define it, and use it in a sentence.

2. Spell *deluge*, and tell students that it means "a great flood." Ask a volunteer to use the word in a sentence. Tell students they will play a game using these same three steps, but they will use a vocabulary (or spelling) list they have been studying.

3. Group students into "ships," or teams of three. Instruct teams to stand together as a group in different locations around the classroom. Give each team a supply of small paper squares or index card halves.

4. Explain that each team will receive five total vocabulary words, one for each turn. During each turn, one student (or "crewmember") spells the word, one defines it, and the third uses the word in a sentence. Each ship's "crew" can determine who will complete which task for each word.

5. Encourage teams to work together so crewmembers are performing using their best skills. For example, if one student is unsure of a definition but knows how to spell a word easily, then that student should spell the word. Alternately, if a student is good with creating sentences, he or she should complete that task.

6. One by one, tell each team their five words. Teams collaborate to write the spelling, the definition, and the sentence for all five words on their paper squares (or "lifesavers"). If a team gets stuck during a turn, they may choose to look at one of their lifesavers for help. They can only use a lifesaver once during a game to save their ship from sinking.

7. The first time a crewmember can't remember how to complete his or her task, he or she may use a lifesaver. But the next time, that player must sit down. A ship "sinks" (or a team is eliminated) when all three crewmembers are seated. As long as they are answering correctly, two players or even one player may keep the ship afloat.

8. When the crew answers correctly, they point to another "ship" to take a turn. Play continues until only one ship remains afloat.

9. Play one or two practice rounds with one team. Point out the fast pace of the game, as teams only have 15 seconds to respond. Explain that you will be timing each turn.

10. Play the game several times or as many times as it takes to review relevant vocabulary or spelling words. After the game, encourage students to add the words and definitions to their writing journals.

Extended Learning

Have students use this game for reviewing other concepts. Ask students to think of three things they would like to learn about this concept, for example, *metaphor*. They may also play this game with literature. For example, players must give three specific facts about a character or setting from a novel.

Answer Key

CONTEXT CLUE CAPERS (PAGES 10–11)

1. giddy–dizzy and lighthearted
2. melancholy–gloomy and thoughtful
3. regicide–the killing of a king
4. admonish–to scold or criticize
5. insipid–having no flavor or taste
6. allusion–a reference to mythology, history, or literature
7. apathetic–not interested or concerned
8. guffaw–a loud burst of laughter
9. plagiarize–to copy and use someone else's ideas and pass them off as your own
10. amend–to correct faults

SENTENCE SHUFFLE (PAGE 57)

1. During the Middle Ages, the plague destroyed one-third of the population in Europe, and it probably delayed the discovery of the New World by approximately 200 years.
2. Fleas carried the disease from rodents to people; however, most people believed the disease was a punishment from God.
3. People were absolutely terrified of the disease, and they left their homes standing empty, their children or parents unburied, and their jobs without notice.
4. Symptoms of the plague included the following: purple boils in the armpits, high fever, vomit with blood, and finally death in three days.
5. Because there were so few workers left, servants and serfs were able to ask for higher wages and better working conditions.
6. The plague, also called the Black Death, killed a massive portion of Europe's population, which led to changes in trade, music, art, and many other things.

PARAGRAPH SHUFFLE (PAGE 58)

One of baseball's favorite legends is that of famous New York Yankee, Babe Ruth, "calling the shot." According to the story, the crowds during that third game of the 1932 World Series were heckling Ruth by throwing lemons and calling him names. What happened next, some say, is remarkable. Ruth got up to bat, pointed his finger toward the center field bleachers, and smacked a home run in the same place he had pointed. However, according to the pitcher, Charlie Root, Ruther never pointed at the bleachers before he swung. Other Chicago Cub team member claimed that Ruth pointed to the players who were taunting him, not the place where the ball was to land. Film evidence does indeed show that Babe Ruth pointed before that famous swing, although it is not clear where he was actually aiming.

CAP IT! RELAY (PAGES 68–69)

1. In April 1912, the *Titanic* sailed from Southampton, England, to Cherbourg, France, and finally to Queenstown, Ireland, to pick up the many millionaires who were to board the ship.
2. Colonel John Jacob Aster, famous for owning real estate in Manhattan, including the famous Waldorf Astoria Hotel, sailed with his dog Kitty and was among the most famous first-class travelers aboard the *Titanic*.
3. Isidor Straus, who served as a U.S. Congressman and was a mentor to Grover Cleveland, was another millionaire who made his fortune in New York City. He started a glassware business in the corner of Macy's department store.
4. Isidor's wife Ida refused to leave her husband and stayed aboard the *Titanic* on that fateful Saturday night. She then gave her fur coat to her maid stating, "It will be cold in the lifeboat."
5. Harry Widener had traveled to Europe to add to his book collection and had purchased a rare edition of a book by Sir Francis Bacon; however, neither he nor his text survived.
6. Benjamin Guggenheim, a Swiss American, stands out from the other millionaires aboard the White Star Line ship. He changed into his formal evening clothes before the *Titanic* sank, apparently so he could die looking like a gentleman.
7. Margaret Brown, otherwise known as the "Unsinkable Molly Brown," had met New York's elite couple, J. J. Astor and his wife Madeleine, on an Egyptian vacation.
8. When Molly Brown's husband heard she had survived the *Titanic*, he exclaimed, "She's too mean to sink!"
9. Guglielmo Marconi, another passenger, invented the wireless telegraph that was used to call out the S.O.S. signals to the rescuing ship, the *Carpathia*.
10. The *Titanic* hit an iceberg in the North Atlantic Sea approximately 400 miles from Newfoundland. Many of the millionaire travelers were saved, while virtually none of the third-class passengers lived.

ERROR BEARERS (PAGE 79)

1. In Medieval times, the standard of beauty was different than today's. Errors: 5
2. Women who had large foreheads and clear skin were considered more attractive. Errors: 3
3. Some ladies plucked out the hair around their foreheads to make them look larger. Errors: 3
4. Many women liked men who were heavy because they believed they were rich and could afford to eat. Errors: 2
5. A huge part of the population had small pox; many people had scars on their faces, so those who escaped the disease were lucky. Errors: 5
6. Medieval society also admired people who had all of the their teeth, because many lost teeth due to decay, a lack of toothbrushes, and the ignorance of dentists. Errors: 3
7. Onions and garlic were the most popular vegetables, therefore people's breath smelled unpleasant. Errors: 3
8. Because people believed that dirt on skin kept away diseases, most peasants took baths only once a year. Errors: 4
9. There was no such thing as deodorant. Soap was made of fat. Errors: 2
10. Yuck! People who lived during this time period cleaned their garments with lard. Errors: 3
11. In The Canterbury Tales, a book by Geoffrey Chaucer, a woman was considered beautiful if she had gapped teeth. Errors: 4
12. Aren't you glad you didn't live back then? Errors: 1

References

Beers, K. (2000). Reading skills and strategies: Reaching reluctant readers. In *Elements of literature series: Grades 6–12*. Austin: TX: Holt, Rinehart and Winston.

Beyers, J. (1998). The biology of human play. *Child Development, 69*(3), 599–600.

Blake, W. (1982). *The complete poetry and prose of William Blake* (Rev. ed.). Berkeley, CA: University of California Press.

Cushman, C. (2005). *Catherine, called Birdy*. New York, NY: Harper Trophy.

Dictionary.com. (n.d.). *Online etymology dictionary*. Retrieved March 26, 2007, from http://dictionary.reference.com.

Frances, G., & Gies, J. (1979). *Life in a medieval castle*. New York, NY: Harper Perennial.

Funk, W. (1992). *Word origins: An exploration and history of words and language* (Reprint ed.). San Antonio, TX: Wings Press.

Gardner, H. (1983). *Frames of mind: The theory of multiple intelligences*. New York, NY: Basic Books.

Hinton, S. E. (2003). *The outsiders* (Rev. ed.). London, England: Puffin Books.

Jensen, E. (2001). *Arts with the brain in mind*. Alexandria, VA: Association for Supervision and Curriculum Development.

McCarthy, B. (1990). Using the 4MAT system to bring learning styles to schools. *Educational Leadership, 48*(2), 31–37.

Memorial University of Newfoundland. (n.d.). *Tales collected by the Brothers Grimm*. Retrieved May 20, 2007, from http://www.ucs.mun.ca/~wbarker/fairies/grimm/.

Nash, O. (n.d.). *The purist*. Retrieved May 20, 2007, from the PoemHunter.com Web site: http://poemhunter.com/poem/the-purist.

National Council of Teachers of English and International Reading Association. (1996). *Standards for the English language arts*. Urbana, IL: National Council of Teachers of English (NCTE).

Noyes, A. (2006). *The highwayman*. New York, NY: Oxford University Press.

Rawls, W. (2000). *Where the red fern grows*. New York, NY: Yearling.

RickWalton.com. (n.d.). *2,276 compound words*. Retrieved February 27, 2007, from www.rickwalton.com/curricul/compound.htm.

Rutman, S., & Stevenson, J. (1998). *The complete idiot's guide to the Titanic*. New York, NY: Alpha Books.

Shakespeare, W. (2003). *Macbeth*. (B. A. Mowat & P. Werstine, Eds.). New York, NY: Washington Square Press.

Shakespeare, W. (2004). *A midsummer night's dream*. (B. A. Mowat & P. Werstine, Eds.). New York, NY: Washington Square Press.

Silverstein, S. (2003). Sick. In *Where the sidewalk ends*. New York, NY: HarperCollins Children's Books.

Tate, M. L. (2003). *Worksheets don't grow dendrites: 20 instructional strategies that engage the brain*. Thousand Oaks, CA: Corwin Press.

Thesaurus.com. (n.d.). *Roget's new millennium thesaurus* (1st ed., Vol. 1.3.1). Retrieved February 23, 2007, from http://thesaurus.reference.com/browse.

Wikipedia: The Free Encyclopedia. (n.d.). *Melodrama*. Retrieved March 11, 2007, from http://en.wikipedia.org/w/index.php?title=Melodrama&oldid=11793072.

Wolfe, P. (2001). *Brain matters: Translating research into classroom practice*. Alexandria, VA: Association for Supervision and Curriculum Development.